A Time of Innocence

A Time of Innocence

A Punderful Memoir of Childhood

William Van Osdol, MD

Copyright © 2019 William Van Osdol, MD
All rights reserved
ISBN: 9781081662196

Dedication

In loving memory of my dear Mom and Dad, who inspired me to become the person I am today.

Childhood is a time of innocence
It is the morning of life when all is change and wonder
It begins with being born and ends with growing up.
-Joan Walsh Anglund-

There was a child went forth every day:
And the first object he look'd upon, that object he became;
And that object became part of him for the day, or a certain
part of the day, or for many years, or stretching cycles of years.
-Walt Whitman-

A pun is the lowest form of wit,
It does not tax the brain a bit.
-Samuel Johnson-

Puns don't get no respect.
-Rodney Dangerfield (paraphrase)-

Times are bad. Children no longer obey their
parents and everyone is writing a book.
-Cicero, 43 BC-

I'm sorry, but how can one possible pay attention to a book with no pictures in it?
-Alice in Wonderland-

Cartoon courtesy of Shannon Wheeler

Acknowledgements

First, I want to thank Our Lord for giving me the wisdom and strength to write this memoir.

I am deeply grateful to my dear, loving wife, Barbie. She has always encouraged me to write about my childhood experiences, and has given me tremendous support and excellent suggestions during the many long hours I spent writing this book. Barbie, thank you so much—you are awesome and amazing.

I want to express my gratitude and appreciation for the incredible help in recalling family memories that I received from my precious siblings, Sister Sara, Susie, Mary Pat, Margie, and Tom.

I also want to thank my dear sons, Adam and Aaron, for the loving encouragement they have given me in writing this memoir.

I am thankful indeed for the great assistance in remembering childhood events that I received from many of my cherished friends who grew up with me: Bob Phillips, Ed Huffer, Kevin Smyth, Dave Delp, Don Pittenger, Bill Hoover, and Sally (Webb) Amstutz. Our wonderful childhood memories will now live on.

In addition, I would like to thank my fellow punsters and pun pals for their punderful inspiration: Pete Townes, Stan Schenher, Peter Wiethe, Steve Heimann, and Tom Funk. Remember, time flies when you are having pun, time flies like an arrow, and fruit flies like bananas.

I owe a special debt to another dear friend, Kathy Fox, for her helpful suggestions and constructive criticism.

I would also like to give a special thanks to my esteemed friends Pete Townes, Tom Alsop and Jill Alsop for their incredible editing and technical assistance, and for helping me finally get this book published.

I feel I must also thank all of my family and friends for putting up with my often terrible puns and jokes over the years … you are all very dear to my heart. I truly love and appreciate all of you.

Last (but not leash), I cannot forget to thank my dog, Mon Chéri. Without her, this book never would have been bitten, although she may have been acting critically.

When it comes to puns, I am especially grateful to the creators of the movie *Airplane*, and Shirley you know why. I do wish Siri would stop calling me Shirley, though, when I leave my cell phone in Airplane mode.

I have a terrible disease in which I cannot stop telling jokes about airplanes and airports. The doctor says it's terminal.

Lastly, I would like to thank my legs for always supporting me, my arms for always being by my side, and especially my fingers and toes because I know I can always count on them.

Table of Contents

Chapter 1: Once Up Pun a Time 1
Chapter 2: What the Dickens? 7
Chapter 3: Woods, Harry's Hole, Split Rock, and Garden 9
Chapter 4: Cow Pasture, Indian Hill, and Ford Lake 15
Chapter 5: Brown House, Log Cabin, Playhouse, and Shed 17
Chapter 6: Secret Clubs and Hideouts 22
Chapter 7: Beyer's Farm 32
Chapter 8: Sacraments, Catechism, Church, and God 34
Chapter 9: Mischief and Misadventures 43
Chapter 10: Pranks and High Jinks 47
Chapter 11: Getting Along Together 54
Chapter 12: Indoor Games, Toys, and Activities 56
Chapter 13: Outdoor Games, Toys, and Activities 62
Chapter 14: Adventures 74
Chapter 15: Chores 80
Chapter 16: Baseball, Hot Dogs, Apple Pie, and Chevrolets 82
Chapter 17: Basketball 99
Chapter 18: Football 103
Chapter 19: Golf and Tennis 109
Chapter 20: Young Writers 112
Chapter 21: Dogs 118
Chapter 22: Candy, Gum, Cracker Jacks, and Ice Cream 122
Chapter 23: Souvenirs, Novelties, and Pop 126
Chapter 24: Ballads, Poems, Plays, and Pantomimes 129
Chapter 25: Family Vacations 131
Chapter 26: Dining Room and New Room 140
Chapter 27: The Eye Doctor 145
Chapter 28: Fishing, Swimming, and Lake Cottages 147
Chapter 29: Books, Magazines and Newspapers 156
Chapter 30: Radio and TV 164
Chapter 31: The Milkman 169

Chapter 32: Movies 171
Chapter 33: Songs, Singers, Records and Music 176
Chapter 34: Nursery Rhymes and Fairy Tales 181
Chapter 35: Charles Atlas, Jiu Jitsu, Popeye, and Bosco 183
Chapter 36: Ovaltine and Captain Midnight............................. 187
Chapter 37: Breakfast Cereals and Eggs 190
Chapter 38: Doctors and Red Medicine 194
Chapter 39: The County Fair 197
Chapter 40: Holidays 200
Chapter 41: Downtown 212
Chapter 42: Hobbies and Pastimes 219
Chapter 43: Summer Jobs.. 225
Chapter 44: My Grandparents.. 229
Chapter 45: My Aunts, Uncles, and Cousins 233
Chapter 46: My Parents in Early Years 238
Chapter 47: My Parents in Later Years.. 247
Chapter 48: My Sisters 259
Chapter 49: My Brothers 278
Chapter 50: West Wayne and East Wayne 293
Chapter 51: Junior High School.. 304
Chapter 52: High School.. 311
Chapter 53: Loss of Innocence 327
Appendix A: Radio Broadcast.. 331
Appendix B: Favorite Recipes 332
Appendix C: The Ballad of Johnny Sands 335
Appendix D: Thanksgiving Day at the Kiefers......................... 336
Appendix E: Excerpts from Mommy's Journal......................... 339
Endnotes 341
Bibliography... 352
Postcard Reproductions 356

Introduction

This is the story of my childhood during the 1940s and 1950s, a time that has been called the "Last Age of Innocence."[1]

Life then seemed simple, safe, unhurried, and peaceful. Families were close-knit and would do most things together, such as dining at home, going on outings, praying, and attending church. Moms usually stayed home, cleaned, and cooked. There were few fast food restaurants and most families did not eat out often.

There were no cell phones, video games, computers, emails or microwaves. Some families had TVs, but kids were not allowed to watch for long hours; instead, they spent most of their time playing outside, rain or shine, where every day brought a new adventure. When kids were inside, they often listened to the radio, played board games, or did their homework.

People didn't have to lock their doors, and neighborhoods were safe at night. There was not much of a drug problem, and little drinking among teenagers.

Kids, for the most part, were happy then. They learned right from wrong, usually obeyed their parents, and respected their teachers. Parents were strict and children were often spanked if they did misbehave.

Somehow kids managed to survive toy guns, second-hand smoke, sugar-coated cereals, and lead paint, not to mention the absence of seat belts, bike helmets, sunscreens, and hand sanitizers.

It was a time of soda fountains, five-and-ten stores, ice cream parlors, candy stores, and drive-in restaurants. Rock-and-roll music, sock hops, juke boxes, 45 rpm records, hot rods, and going steady were teenage crazes.

Boys had flat top and duck tail haircuts, and girls had pony tails. Fashion trends for teenage boys included pegged pants, rolled-up sleeves, and leather jackets, while the girls wore bobby socks, saddle shoes, and poodle skirts.

Kids idolized (and couldn't get enough of) Elvis Presley, Ricky Nelson, James Dean, and Marilyn Monroe.

Baseball was America's pastime. Joe DiMaggio and Mickey Mantle were our baseball heroes, and the Yankees usually won the World Series.

After World War II ended, it was a time of peace and prosperity in our country. It was not a perfect time, though. We worried that Russia might attack us, and many people even built bomb shelters. We had a very high poverty rate and segregation in most schools in the South. Most kids got the measles, chicken pox and mumps, and there was a terrible polio epidemic. There was a widespread belief that cigarettes were "cool," and many celebrities, including movie stars and baseball players, promoted smoking.

Overall, though, it was a glorious era. It seemed that the grass was greener, the skies were bluer, the days were sunnier, and life was simply better. As the lyrics from a song go, "Life was slow and oh, so mellow."[2] It was indeed a time when we loved God, our country, baseball, hot dogs, apple pie, and Chevrolets.

This memoir of my childhood, which consists of anecdotes and recollections (often humorous and joyful, but sometimes sad), begins when I was born. It will take you through my early journey during the forties and fifties, as I grew, matured, gradually overcame some of my awkwardness and shyness, came of age, and lost my innocence.

As my story unfolds, you will be introduced to my family, friends, teachers, and others who shared my life and influenced me along the way.

You will notice that I have referred to my dear parents by the several names we all knew them by—"Mommy" and "Daddy" when we were young, and then sometimes "Mom" and "Dad" as we grew older. (Although, even today, we still often lovingly remember them as "Mommy" and "Daddy.")

We always called our beloved grandparents "Mamaw" and "Pappy," and that is reflected throughout the book.

You will also notice that I have referred to my precious brothers and sisters by the various names we knew them by as they grew older—Sara Joan was first called "Sally Jo" and then "Sally" or "Sister Sara," Susan Jane became "Susie" or "Sue," Thomas Dean was first called "Tommy" and then "Tom," John Anthony was always called "Tony," Mary Patricia was mostly called "Mary Pat" (although we sometimes called her just "Mary"), and Margaret Ellen was always "Margie." My given name was William Russell, but I was always called "Billy" or "Bill" (although sometimes Daddy called me "Willy").

Some of these anecdotes and recollections may differ slightly from the actual events, but they have been written as I remember them, or as I may have been told about them. At times I have left out names to protect identities. My only regret is that I cannot remember even more details about this wonderful and adventurous time of my life.

Now, I readily admit that I am an avowed and unabashed punster and jokester. I believe I have my Daddy's great sense of humor to thank at least partly for all of that. (I didn't like puns so much when I was younger, but I have groan to love them over the years...)

So for your reading pleasure, I have taken it up pun myself to add a corny-copia of humorous comments, jokes, and puns throughout this memoir. After all, the only risk in writing bad puns would be pun-itive damages. My doctor told me there was only one cure for telling too many puns, and that was to give me a shot of punicillin.

Please note that these aforementioned humorous comments, jokes, and puns have been written in **bold letters,** to make clear to the readers that these entries should not be considered actual parts of my anecdotes and recollections.

You will also notice that most of this memoir is written in the past tense. When I have sometimes changed to the present tense to make an editorial comment, that section is in *italics*.

My purpose in writing this memoir has been to give my children, grandchildren, nephews, nieces, and any other descendants a legacy that is a glimpse of my life at a different and more innocent time, and to show them how my childhood may have been unlike theirs. I have also wished to entertain and bring back fond memories to my dear brothers and sisters, to my cherished friends who grew up with me, and to others who experienced this era or may otherwise have an interest in this memorable time.

Writing this memoir has been an immense pleasure and a labor of love for me. I truly hope that you will enjoy it as much as I have enjoyed writing it.

Chapter 1: Once Up Pun a Time

I was born on my birthday, at a very young age, on a day that may go down in infamy, at McDonald Hospital in Warsaw, Indiana, in 1942.
The room next to me was 1943.

McDonald Hospital

Before I was born, I thought I was having a midwife crisis. Although I didn't want to be ovary-acting, I had been inside so long that it seemed like a maternity. Water you supposed to do when your head is swimming, you feel tied down, your world has turned upside down, you are suffering from separation anxiety, and you are running out of womb?

When I heard people saying words such as, "Don't, can't, won't, I'm, and shouldn't," I thought, "Oh, no! The contractions are starting!" I knew then that it was time to be born. So at the break of day, I headed out into this world, and my OB doctor, OB Wan Kenobi, said to me, "May the farce be with you!"

As soon as I was born, I was hungry, and since I was still at McDonalds, I asked for a cordless phone to call for womb cervix so I could order a Big Mac.

I was not the cutest baby ever...the stork flew backwards so he didn't have to look at me, and after I was born the nurses went down to the zoo and threw rocks at the stork. I was such a big baby, on a scale of 1-10, that they thought I would have to be delivered by a crane instead of a stork. My doctor, Dr. Baum, nearly exploded when he saw me.

Someone even sent my baby picture to "Ripley's Believe It or Not." Robert Ripley sent it back and said, "I don't believe it."

Soon after I was born, a different doctor took blood from my jocular vein, and tests showed my jinks were too high. So he performed surgery on me by replacing my humorous with a funny bone.

Make no bones about it, though, I had a bone to pick with that doctor. Tibia honest, although my doctor was working himself to the bone, I am not sure he was a bone-a-fide doctor, and I marrowly survived the surgery. I could feel it in my bones that this was because the doctor was working with ulna a skeleton crew.

Not long after I was born, our family at the time, which included Sally Jo, Susan Jane, Tommy, Mommy, Daddy, and I, moved from our home on Union Street downtown into a larger home in a dense woods on the outside edge of Warsaw.

Our new home was a cozy, one-story dwelling with white, wood siding and red shutters, a small, concrete front porch, an unfinished basement, and a spacious attic. Daddy had the garage made into a bedroom before we moved in; then we had three bedrooms, one bathroom, a dining room, a kitchen, and a living room with a beautiful stone fireplace.

A Time of Innocence

Our home in the woods

I slept in a wooden baby cradle that Mommy had bought just before I was born. She told us later that the cradle had been used by the famous Mayo Clinic brothers.

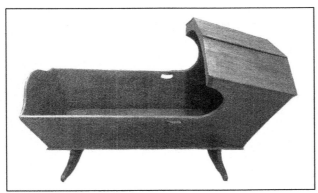

The cradle I slept in

Later I called the Mayo Clinic. I wanted to talk to Dr. Mayo to see if I could find a Clue about the old cradle—wooden you? I talked to someone named Colonel Mustard, who was in the library, and Mr. Green who was in the lounge. They said they could help, but that they weren't playing games with me. Colonel Mustard did give me a Clue about Dr. Mayo when he

said that he didn't want to throw a wrench in the works, but that it was a lead-pipe cinch that Mayo was still dressing after surgery. Then Mr. Green said, "Please don't kale the messenger, but lettuce all romaine calm and leaf it to me, and oil spread the word to hold the Mayo until we can ketchup with him."

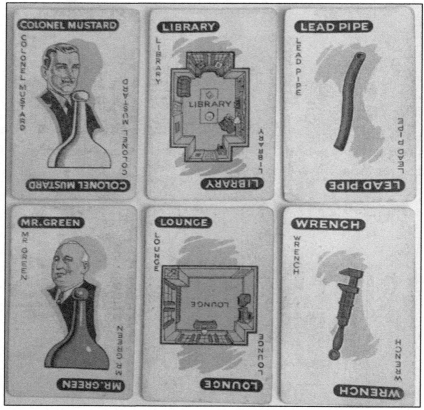

Clues to solving the cradle mystery—from the game Clue

Our country was still fighting in World War II in my early years. We had to use ration books with stamps to buy some items like sugar, coffee, meat, and canned goods.

It would have been irrational if we didn't use the stamps.

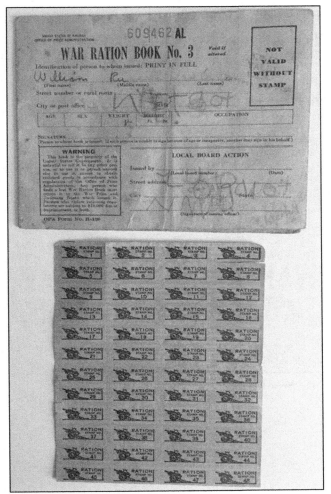

My war ration book and stamps

Our Presidents in my early years were Franklin D. Roosevelt, Harry S. Truman and Dwight D. "Ike" Eisenhower. Daddy especially liked Truman. He sometimes called him, "Give 'Em Hell, Harry!"

It was always said that the "S" in Harry S. Truman's name did not actually stand for anything.

The rumor was pasta around, though, that someone had accidentally dropped a piece of spaghetti on his birth certificate.

One of my earliest memories was when I was about three years old. I vaguely remember hearing people excitedly saying that the war was finally over.

World War II was over

Chapter 2: What the Dickens?

It was the best of times. It was the wurst of times.

Why was it the wurst of times? To be frank, although I may have been a cute little Dickens when I was young, everyone said that it couldn't be furter from the truth and it was just baloney that I was ever innocent. People said they never sausage a spoiled brat, and that I could even be the missing link in evolution.

And to be Frank, I would have to change my name. Speaking of Frank, you should meat his grill-friend Pattie; they're engaged to be marinated.

You may not know this, but Charles Dickens wrote a classic historical novel about two sofas in London and Paris. The book was called *A Tale of Two Settees*.

Charles Dickens

That reminds me of a butcher in London who caught a big sea creature in the river there and turned it into sausage. It was the beast of Thames, it was the wurst of Thames. Sometimes the butcher had to carry the sausage around in his suitcase, but that was the wurst-case scenario.

I could also tell you about the time I was in Paris and jumped in the river there, but you might think I was in Seine.

Once up pun a thyme, when Charles Dicken's wife cooked for him, she used all grades of thyme in her sausage. It was the best of thyme, it was the wurst of thyme.

Maybe I have too much thyme on my hands, but I am having the thyme of my life writing these puns. Now, though, it is thyme to move on or I might spend thyme in the punitentiary.

Just as Celine Dijon mustard up her voice—this feels like Dijon vu all over again—and became an Oscar wiener, (I downloaded the song from "Titanic"—it is sinking right now—and yes, I have sunk to a new low with this pun), I now relish the thought of telling my story and becoming the top dog of memoir writers. So be prepared, because the wurst is yet to come.

Chapter 3: Woods, Harry's Hole, Split Rock, and Garden

The woods we lived in, about eight acres of land, were both our playground and our haven while we were growing up. We spent most of our summer days there exploring and enjoying exciting adventures. We made trails and hideouts, climbed trees, camped, and had picnics in the woods.

When it was time to come in and eat supper (it was not called dinner back then), Mommy loudly rang the Indian brass bells that were hanging in our dining room, and then we all came running back into the house.

Our Indian brass bells

When spring came, our woods were filled with glorious pink and white blossoms on the trees, beautiful wildflowers that included buttercups and violets, and the umbrella-like leaves of the mayapples nestled in the shade.

Mayapples

Me holding vase of buttercups

    I liked to gather bouquets of yellow buttercups and give them to Mommy. She would lovingly put them in a small vase.

    We enjoyed listening to the singing and chirping of the many birds in our woods. They included robins, blue jays, sparrows, bobwhites, cardinals, and red-headed woodpeckers with their familiar rat-tat-tat.

A Time of Innocence

I especially liked to hear the first robins singing in the spring.

On sunny days when there are Baskin Robbins, ice cream if I see a cat attacking them.

We loved the familiar sights, sounds, and smells of our woods in the summertime—the narrow and winding trails, the overgrown and tangled weeds, the dense green foliage of the stately trees, the delicate flitting butterflies, the wild blackberry, boysenberry and raspberry bushes, the sweet fragrance of the mayapple fruit, the dense patches of goldenrods, the pod-like fruit of the milkweeds, the many yellow dandelions, and the sun-kissed black-eyed Susans.

Most of the trees in our woods were tall oaks, maples, redbuds, sycamores, and shagbark hickories. I liked climbing them, particularly the maples, as the branches were lower and easier to climb.

There was a redbud tree in our backyard next to the playhouse. We especially liked to climb that tree and carve our initials in the bark.

We had a lot of mulberry trees in our woods. The ground was always thoroughly messy where the berries fell off these trees. We didn't usually eat the mulberries.

There was also a sassafras tree that we found growing back in the woods. One day we decided that we wanted to make root beer and sassafras tea from the tree. We cut out a piece of the root that we could use. We saved that root for a long time, but we never got around to making root beer or sassafras tea with it.

The root of the matter was that sassafras was just not our cup of tea.

There were rhubarb and raspberry bushes growing in the garden behind the house. We had wild strawberries growing in our backyard, and we would sometimes pick and eat them when we were playing.

We also gathered ground cherries growing along the side of the road. They were hard to find. They fell on the ground when they were ripe, and the cherries were inside golden husks. Our grandma, Mamaw, made the most delicious pies from them.

We had a little orchard along the back fence, but we never got much fruit from the trees.

It would have been fruitless to try.

Fireflies would light up the night as we listened to the chirping of the katydids and crickets, and the hoots of majestic owls.

When you hear that we had owls in our woods, you might say, "Well, owl be!", or you could say, "Who-o-o gives a hoot!"

We loved all the wildlife in our woods, including rabbits, squirrels, foxes, skunks, possums, and raccoons.

I know there were otter animals, I just can't think of their names.

We tried to avoid the many stinging nettle weeds that grew in the woods. If you touched them, you would soon break out in a painful, itchy rash. We learned, though, that if we rubbed dirt on the rash, it usually made the rash feel better.

In the fall, our woods became ablaze with colors of orange, yellow, and red. Soon the woods were filled with many leaves fluttering down from the trees, and the ground became strewn with layers of the crackling, fallen leaves. We then began to smell the decaying leaves as they crunched under our feet. Smoke from burning leaves in the surrounding countryside filled the air with a pleasant aroma. It would not be long before our bare trees would again be exposed to the cold chills of winter.

Our favorite place to play in the woods was Harry's Hole. Rather obviously, we named it after a man named Harry, who had started to build a house there and had dug a large hole for the basement. For some reason, Harry decided not to build the house after all and left the hole there with big piles of dirt around it. Our parents later bought that end of the woods from him.

A Time of Innocence

We spent a lot of time one summer digging a deep hole in the middle of Harry's Hole. We thought if we dug deep enough, we might strike a well. We wanted to make a lake so that we could go fishing and swimming. Although we dug down about 6 feet, we never did find water.

There were raspberries, blackberries, and boysenberries growing around Harry's Hole. These all made delicious pies.

Harry's Hole was also a great place to go sledding and to have picnics, club meetings, and hideouts.

Another favorite place to meet in the woods had a large rock with a split in it, so of course, we named the place Split Rock. We built campfires and had picnics and club meetings there. We thought it was probably a place where Indians had once met to have campfires.

Since there was a big clearing there, we were able to have a vegetable garden at that end of the woods, far from the house. We had to carry water in buckets in order to water the garden, and the sun was really hot there.

We all looked a little pail after carrying those buckets of water.

The ground there was mostly clay and was as hard as a rock. That often made it almost impossible to cultivate. It was worth it in the end, however; that garden produced a lot of really delicious green beans, sweet corn, tomatoes, and other vegetables.

You could say that the end justified the beans.

There could be a kernel of truth that puns about corn might go in one ear and out the other, and this may sound corny, but, shucks, you don't have to stalk me to get me to write them. I will see hominy puns about corn I can write. If you know any other puns about corn, I'm all ears.

Although good vegetable puns can be hard to find, I herb that sometimes a good vegetable pun will just crop up, although they don't turnip very often. Still some vegetable puns are hard

to beet, even though you might not carrot all. I do try to keep my eyes peeled for good puns about potatoes. I've liked tater puns since I was a tot.

Soy lettuce not forget that these vegetable puns are just the tip of the iceberg, and many more romaine in my head. Rosemary, although I had not met herbivore, gave me sage advice, and said these puns were a long thyme cumin. Sometimes I like to write them just to kale time, or just to be garden my reputation to produce them. I really shouldn't leek this, but I don't make a very good celery writing these puns, and I don't want my wages to be garnished.

We grew asparagus inside a wire fence and covered it with canvas, which was the awning of the cage of asparagus.

But I've bean thinking that if you need some peas and quiet, it's not a big dill and I will stop writing these vegetable puns. I do hope, though, that I don't get a black-eye over my pun about peas.

I yam tired anyway. I will just leaf in my V8 juiced up hot rod, and go be a couch potato and watch YouTuber and my favorite TV show, Okra Winfrey. It's my wife's birthday anyway, and I have to cauliflower shop. After that, because I am beet, I just want to go home, read the pepper, turnip the sheets, endive into bed.

Chapter 4: Cow Pasture, Indian Hill, and Ford Lake

Further back from our woods, there was a cow pasture where we liked to climb the old wooden fence next to the sycamores and Osage orange trees and play in the pasture. Sometimes there were cows and bulls in the pasture. We tried to stay away from them.

One time when we were playing in the cow pasture with our friends Eddie and Billy Huffer, we found a fresh cow patty. Tommy threw a big rock on it, and poop splattered all over Billy Huffer's pants.

On the other side of the pasture was a marsh that had a little pond where we would ice skate in the winter. The pond was part of a winding creek that ran from Pike Lake over past Beyer's farm.

On the far side of the marsh was a larger pond that had an old Model T Ford in it, so we called it Ford Lake. In the wintertime, we sometimes ice skated or played hockey on Ford Lake.

Not far from the lake was an old empty cellar. The cellar was near the road we called Dalton's Lane, since it went back to Betsy Dalton's house.

Betsy was one of Susan Jane's best friends. Susan Jane (one of my older sisters) and Betsy used to ride double on Betsy's horse, Scotty. They rode up and down Dalton's Lane, on the hilly grounds by the side of the lane and the country roads.

Past Ford Lake was a big hill overlooking Oakwood Cemetery and Pike Lake. It was said that the cemetery was on an old Indian burial ground. We called the place Indian Hill, and we liked to play and have picnics there.

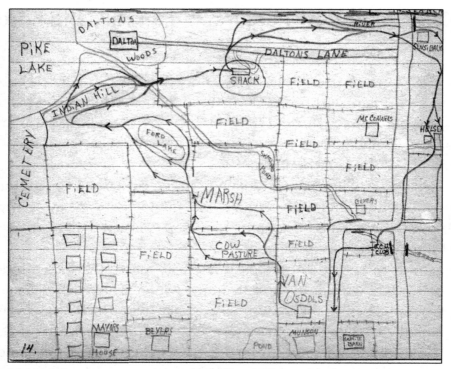

Map of the cow pasture, marsh, Indian Hill, Ford Lake, Dalton's Lane, Pike Lake, Beyer's farm, and our house. Illustration from the book, *The Van Osdol's Adventures,* by Tom Van Osdol.

I'll never forget those childhood summers, when we would climb inside old tires and roll down the hill. They were Goodyears.

Chapter 5: Brown House, Log Cabin, Playhouse, and Shed

Other places where we played in our back yard were the brown house, the little log cabin, the playhouse, and the old shed.

The brown house had been a one-car garage in the town of Winona Lake before we bought it and had it moved to our backyard. It had windows, two doors, brown wooden siding, and a dark attic. We used it to store tools, lawn mowers, toys, and sports equipment. We had old bunk beds in the brown house that we bought at an auction, and sometimes we slept there all night. Although we had to stand on a ladder to get up in the attic, it made a really good hideout.

Brown house, trailer, and playhouse with squirrel in foreground

The playhouse had white wooden siding and red shutters and was about 4 x 6 feet in size. Mary Pat and Margie (my younger sisters) liked to play with their dolls and have tea parties in the playhouse, and take naps in there, as well. It also made a good hideout or a meeting place for our clubs.

Playhouse. (L-R) Billy Fagaly, Susan Jane, Sally Jo, and Patty Fagaly

We had a small log cabin behind our house. It was about the same size as the playhouse and was always one of our favorite places to play and have picnics. We dug some tunnels under the log cabin, and we were really lucky that none of them ever collapsed. We had planned to use the tunnels for a bomb shelter, in case Russia ever attacked us.

We all liked to play, "Annie-Annie Over," by throwing a ball over the playhouse or the brown house. If the ball didn't go all the way over, you would shout, "Pigtails!" If the person on the other side caught the ball, he would sneak around the building and throw the ball at you. We often played this game by throwing the ball over our house, too. That was even more fun.

The shed was an old, gray, weather-beaten chicken coop that we bought from a farmer. We had it moved to our woods, near the little orchard. We used it to store lawn furniture and other things. It made a good hideout for our clubs.

A Time of Innocence

After we bought the chicken shed, we all got together and hatched an idea to raise chickens there. We knew we had to think out of the boks. A little bird told us that it would be cheep to raise chickens, that it would cost us only a poultry sum to get started, and the money that it would cost would be just chicken feed.

We had a little nest egg to help get us started raising the chickens. We thought it would be a feather in our caps if we could do it, although we did worry that we might lay an egg. We knew we would have to wing it, because we didn't know much about chickens and that we would have to start from scratch—but we still thought we could pullet off.

We decided we wanted to raise cage-free and free range chickens. We even decided to home-school them. We also created a transgender breed of chickens that we called Himalayan.

We bought Tyson chickens from a man named Mike, but we didn't know if they would come in a big boxer not. Then we found out that the Tyson chickens didn't have any ears.

We spent a lot of time tending to our chickens, and, in fact, you might call us chicken tenders. Some of our chickens wanted to get a sitter for their eggs so they could go out at night. It dozen make cents for a chicken to shell out money for a sitter, although it was better than carton the eggs around with them, and eggs are cheeper by the dozen.

It was hard to find good chickens—they were as scarce as hen's teeth—but we had to capon looking. We didn't want to buy any bad chickens, because we were afraid they might lay deviled eggs. When some of our eggs came up missing, we thought it might have been a poacher who took them.

One of our chickens crossed the playground to get to the other slide. The police were going to arrest the chicken because the playground was closed, but they let it slide. Another chicken, who was blunt and direct, went to the middle of the road so it could lay it on the line. One day we thought one of the chickens left the pen, but she was just out on bale.

Some chickens had problems with their eggs rolling everywhere—they must have had restless eggs syndrome. Other chickens were always moving around; you could say it was poultry in motion. One of our chickens was always using bad language because it had a fowl mouth. We tried to get the hens to lay eggs around the cluck, but their eggs were not all they were cracked up to be.

We needed to get answers from our chickens about why they weren't laying more eggs, so although we knew it would be tough on them, we grilled them for hours. We asked questions like, "Who came first, you or the egg?" and "Why did you cross the road?"

It was hard to keep the shed clean, and we were always walking on egg shells when we were around each other. One day in the shed, I tripped and started to fall on one of our chickens, whose name was Chicken Little, and he cried out, "This guy is falling, this guy is falling!"

The chickens must have enjoyed classical music, because when we asked them what kind of music they liked, they all said, "Bach, Bach, Bach!" For some reason, the only kind of movies they liked to watch were chick flicks. They also liked to dance chick-to-chick.

We were having trouble making hens meet. Some of our hens weren't spring chickens anymore, and were getting older and going into henopause. We gave our chickens a bushel of chicken feed, but they only took a peck, and we made a mistake and counted our chickens before they hatched. That put us all in a fowl mood and we shed a few tears. We knew we could not recoop our losses, but we didn't brood or squawk over it.

A Time of Innocence

So we chickened out, and since Colonel Sanders had kicked the bucket, hensforth we sold all our chickens to a psychiatrist, Dr. Sigmund Freud, from Kentucky. Dr. Freud let it slip that he was going to open a Kentucky Freud Chicken franchise.

William R. Van Osdol, MD

Chapter 6: Secret Clubs and Hideouts

We had a lot of secret clubs, including the Three Turtles Club, Bowery Boys Club, Black Arrow Club, Two Creepers Club, Two Braves Club, Aqua Club, Athletic Club, Injun-Uitie Club, Scout Club, Li'l Abner Club, and Dr Pepper Club.

We had many clubhouses and hideouts for these clubs, including the basement by the back wall, the clump of vines by the raspberry bushes, the shed, the log cabin, the brown house, behind the chair in the new room, the thicket by the orchard, the fence at the end of the woods, the attic stairway, the secret room in Pappy's basement (which was at the base of the stairs), the maple tree, the tree in the cornfield, the back bedroom second closet, the bathtub, and the little village of oak trees.

The Three Turtles Club was one of our first clubs. My secret name was Tubby, Tony was Cubby, and Mary Pat was Lubby.

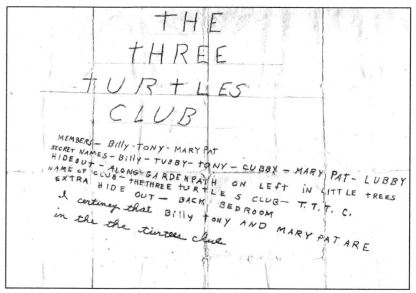

The Three Turtles Club certificate

A Time of Innocence

One of my favorite clubs was the Bowery Boys Club. The clubhouse for the Bowery Boys Club was down in our basement by the back wall. We each had to pay ten cents dues every month to the club. We saved the money from our dues in a little bank, and kept a notebook with the minutes of our meetings. Tom was Mugsy, I was Sach, Tony was Whitey, and Mary Pat was Louie, all characters from the Bowery Boys movies. In those movies, Louie Dumbrowski owned Louie's Sweet Shop, a hangout for the Bowery Boys gang.

The Bowery Boys

The Bowery Boys movie on theater marquee

In the Black Arrow Club, Tommy's secret name was Deadpan and mine was Blackdog. Our password was "Black-out!" and our motto was, "Be strong."

```
Black Arrow Club
Members - Tommy & Billy
Names - Tommy, Deadpan + Billy, Blackdog
Hideout - Log Cabin
Extra Hideout - Up Tree
Password - Black-out!
Mascot - Trees
Motto - Be Strong
Emblem - ⨯
```

The Black Arrow Club certificate

In the Two Creepers Club, Tom's secret name was Sneaker and Tony was Creeper. The motto of the club was, "Be a good sport in all things."

```
            CLUB CERTIFICATE
Club name------ The Two Creepers Club
Hideout-------- Close to old one
Extra hideout-- By Tony's GF hideout (in vines)
Members-------- Tom & Tony
Club names----- Tom, Sneaker-Tony, Creeper
Officers------- Tom                Tony
                President          Vice president
                Treasurer          Vice treasurer
Password------- How (show emblem)
Emblem--------- Picture of somebody crawling or stooping
Mascot--------- Creeping
Motto---------- Be a good sport in all things
Rememberance--- Ecale
                Signed, Tom & Tony
```

The Two Creepers Club certificate

A Time of Innocence

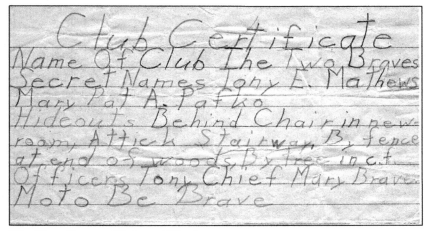

The Two Braves Club certificate

In the Two Braves Club, Tony's secret name was Eddie Mathews and Mary Pat was Andy Pafko. (They were both players on the Milwaukee Braves baseball team.) They had officers in the club, too. Tony was the Chief and Mary Pat was the Brave. The club motto was "Be Brave."

In the Aqua Club, my secret name was Froggy; my club name was Buster Crabbe, a famous Olympic swimmer and actor. Tom's secret name was Flippy; his club name was Johnny Weissmuller, a well-known swimmer who played Tarzan in the movies. Tony's secret name was Goggles; his club name was Joe Verduer, who was an Olympic swimmer. Margie was our mascot; her club name was Marilyn Bell, a long-distance swimmer.

Our Aqua Club motto was, "Don't give up before you've tried"; our colors were aqua and green. Our enemies in the Aqua Club were: #1—The Gill Man, #2—Barracuda, and #3—Shark.

My Aqua Club certificate

In the Athletic Club, Tom's secret name was Bob Mathias and my secret name was Jim Thorpe. Our motto was "Be a sport."

> *Official*
>
> *Club Certificate*
>
> NAME of Club – THE ATHLETIC CLUB (T.A.C.)
> MEMBERS – Tom AND Bill Van Osdol
> SECRET NAMES – Tom, BOB MATHIAS – Bill, JIM THORPE
> Officers – Tom, CAPTAIN – Bill, SERGEANT
> Hideouts – Clump of Vines, By Rasberry Patch – Thicket By Orchard – Attic Stairway – SECRET Room in Pappy's Basement – IN MAPLE TREE – TREE in Cornfield – Back Bed Room 2nd Closet – IN BATHTUB – Little Village of Oak Trees
> Motto – "BE A SPORT"
> PASS-WORD – TACK
> EMBLEM – Picture of ATHLETE Performing and picture of People Shaking Hands.
>
> I CERTIFY THAT Tom Van Osdol AND Billy Van Osdol ARE IN THE ATHLETIC CLUB.

The Athletic Club certificate

The Injun-Uitie Club was named after the Injun-Uities cards that we collected from inside boxes of Nabisco Shredded Wheat cereal. Straight Arrow's "Secrets of Indian Lore and Know-how" were printed on these cards. They included topics such as Indian ponies, bow making, rope hoists, horsemanship, water signals, danger signals, arrow making, rafts, camp fires, and many others.

Injun-Uities from Shredded Wheat boxes

The Injun-Uitie Club certificate

A Time of Innocence

The Injun-Uitie club had a meeting place by the little creek that ran past Beyer's farm in the field across from our house. Susan Jane's club name was Treasure Arrow, Tommy was Comanche Arrow, and I was Swift Arrow. We had secret names in this club, too; Susan Jane's was Silver Arrow, Tommy's was Turquoise Arrow, and I was Golden Arrow. Our motto was "Be Brave," and our password was "Pow-wow!"

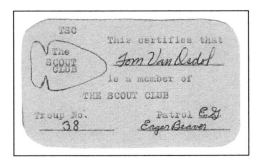

Tom and I started the Scout Club. We called our patrol the Eager Beavers. We made merit badges and had to earn them.

The Scout Club merit badges

In the Li'l Abner Club, I was Li'l Abner and Mary Pat was Daisy Mae. Our motto was, "Be loyal to the club."

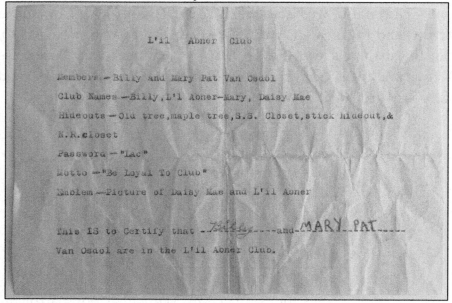

The Li'l Abner Club certificate

Li'l Abner comic book

A Time of Innocence

One time we found an old Dr Pepper bottle on the branch of a tree that we were climbing by the back fence, so we started a Dr Pepper Club. That tree was our hideout for the club.

Dr Pepper soda

Chapter 7: Beyer's Farm

We liked to play in the farm fields around us that were owned by our neighbors, the Beyers. They were good neighbors, but we were always afraid they might catch us when we ran through their fields, played hide-and-seek in the rows of corn, looked for arrowheads, went sledding, or played ice hockey on their frozen ponds.

Susan Jane liked to run through the wheat fields, but Mr. Beyer didn't catch her doing that. However, he did catcher in the rye.

A farmer once thought he had 98 cows on his farm, but when he rounded them up, the number was 100. He should have used a cowculator. He may have made a mistake when he counted the cows, but that's OK, because to err is human, to forgive bovine. Someone may have given him a bum steer, but he didn't want to beef about it. Hay, he shouldn't have a cow over it!

One of the cows liked to veal her oats. She jumped over the barbed wire fence thinking the grass was greener on the other side, and caused udder destruction, but the farmer tractor down.

When one of the cows learned she could read nursery rhymes to the little calves, she was over the moon.

Some of the cows wanted to go on vacation to the Jersey Shore, but they didn't have credit cards to pay for the trip because they were cash cows.

A farmer liked to sing the Beatles song which had the lyrics, "Something in the whey she moos, attracts me like no other udder butter."

You may not like this pun if you are laughtose intolerant, but if you are on a lactose-free diet, it would behoof you to know that cow's feet lactose.

If you veal you've herd this before, you may have deja moo. After their calves were born, the cows drank only decalf coffee.

Some of the calves didn't weigh much when they were born, they were just quarter-pounders. You could always find the calves eating in the calfeteria.

By the way, you can't use "beef stew" as a website password, because it is not stroganoff, and it does not help to beef or stew about it. You should also know that if you are ever in a restaurant and happen to have a cow as your waiter, that cow tipping is not allowed.

You are probably thinking, "Cud you stop it please?" but I will keep writing puns until the cows come home and for heifer and heifer!

Across the road from our house was a clover field. It usually had deep water standing in it after a hard rain. We named the flooded field Clover Lake. We would sometimes take the little green rowboat that Stewart Knox had made for us over to the field and row it around.

There was a little brook running through the clover field.

We couldn't remember the name of that brook, because you can't tell a brook by its clover.

We also liked to look for four-leaf clovers in our yard and in the fields. Sometimes we would find one and get really excited.

We thought about putting the four-leaf clovers that we found between the pages of a book to flatten them, but then we decided not to press our luck.

Chapter 8: Sacraments, Catechism, Church, and God

I was baptized in the old Sacred Heart Catholic Church in Warsaw when I was a few weeks old. Queenie Kiefer was my dear godmother. I never got to know my godfather; his name was James McNeil, and he lived in South Bend.

Sacred Heart Catholic Church

Sacred Heart Catholic Church interior

A Time of Innocence

My godmother, Queenie

I made my first confession at the Sacred Heart Church when I was seven years old. We were supposed to go to confession once a week; though I usually had to confess only a few venial sins, I was always a nervous wreck going to confession.

I still remember my first confession. I said, "Bless me Father for I have sinned...Tommy did it."

I made my first Holy Communion right after that. We had to fast after midnight and drink only water in order to receive communion. When we did receive Holy Communion, we all knelt at the communion rail in front of the altar.

My First Holy Communion. (L-R) Daddy, Susan Jane, me, Mommy, and Sally Jo, with Mary Pat in front

Later I received the sacrament of Confirmation. My confirmation name was Joseph.

We all went to church together every Sunday at Sacred Heart Church. Daddy would usually serve as an usher. We always dressed up for church; my brothers and I wore our best clothes. Mommy and my sisters wore dresses or skirts and something on their heads—either a hat, scarf, or veil. They often wore gloves. Daddy usually wore a suit and tie, and he often wore a hat which he always took off when he entered the church.

Those long dresses and skirts that the women and girls had to wear covered a multitude of shins.

We never missed going to Mass on Sundays and wouldn't even think about eating meat on Fridays.

Parish the thought that we would ever miss Mass on Sundays or eat meat on Fridays.

A Time of Innocence

One of our first parish priests was Father Leo Pursley. He later became Bishop Pursley. He was always a very good friend of our parents.

Bishop Pursley

Father Reddington

Later, our parish priests were Father Mannion and Father Lawrence Reddington. Father Kapphahn was a visiting priest. Sometimes both Father Reddington and Father Kapphahn would come to our home to visit with our parents, and have drinks and talk in the new room. I liked and respected all of our parish priests.[3]

Tommy, Tony, and I were altar boys. We wore white surplices and red cassocks for high Masses, and white surplices with black cassocks for low Masses. Because the masses were said in Latin, we had to learn the Latin responses.

Most of us did not go to a Catholic school, but instead took catechism class in the basement of the rectory or church every Saturday morning.

My catechism book

Nuns were our teachers. The list of nuns included Sister Callista, Sister Mary Martha, and Sister Mary Veronica, from St. John's in Goshen and Victory Noll in Huntington.[4] The sisters were very strict and used clickers in church to let us know when to genuflect or stand up.

I was never very excited about going to those catechism classes on Saturday mornings; I would much rather have been outside playing. Still, I respected all of our nuns and was grateful for them. They taught me all about God and our faith, and to have a strong moral code and conscience.

Some of my friends who went to catechism classes with me were Kevin Smyth, Patty Mulcahy, Susie Lewis, Ronnie Kay, and Kathy Fitzpatrick.

My favorite song at church was, "On This Day, Oh Beautiful Mother."

That song usually brings me to tears now.

After Mass, we loved going down to the church basement with Daddy when the men's club, the Holy Name Society, served breakfast. That was the first time I ever got to drink coffee, which I really liked.

I worried that my parents would ground me if I drank coffee, so words could not espresso how much I loved having that first cup of coffee at church. It meant a latte to me that my Daddy let me have it. After that I tried whatever beans necessary to have another cup of coffee, although sometimes I was a little chai about asking for it.

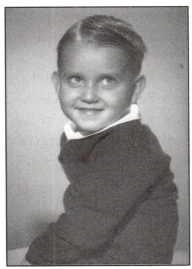

Me at age 4

When I was growing up, I thought a lot about sins, hell, heaven, and God. I worried that if I ever committed a mortal sin, unless I made a good confession, I could go to hell.

When Tony, at age two, said, "Poopy God," I said, "Don't say poopy God, Tony, you won't go to heaven."

When I was five years old, I said, "Daddy, I love God more than I love you." I also said, "I love God more than I do Mary Pat. Do you think she cares?"

Also when I was five, I said, "I see God everywhere, but I can't see him. We shouldn't walk because we might step on God."

We were not supposed to attend a non-Catholic Church, although I always wanted to visit the First Brethren Church. My best friend, Eddie Huffer, attended that church.

On Sunday nights, we would usually all kneel together in the living room to say the rosary. Although my knees would hurt from kneeling, I still loved saying the rosary. One time I said, "Let's say the rosary again. My nose hurts and maybe that will make it better."

Before I went to bed, I usually knelt and said my prayers, including The Lord's Prayer, Hail Mary, Glory Be, Act of Contrition, and Apostles' Creed. Then I would pray for all the souls in purgatory.

I usually wore a blessed scapular medal around my neck. Other Catholic devotionals we had included cloth scapulars, a picture of the Sacred Heart of Jesus (on the wall in our living room), a holy water font (by the front door), relics, crucifixes, rosaries, missals, and a beautiful statue of the Infant Jesus of Prague.

Sacred Heart of Jesus

Infant Jesus of Prague. (Photo copyrighted and courtesy of the League of the Miraculous Infant Jesus of Prague in Darien, Ill.)

In the summer of 1950, Daddy drove us all, except my youngest sister Margie, who hadn't been born yet, up to Necedah, Wisconsin. A woman named Mary Ann Van Hoof said she had been having apparitions from the Blessed Virgin Mary, and that the Virgin Mary was supposed to appear to her again on August 15th at noon.[5]

When we arrived at the farm where Mary Ann Van Hoof lived, there were big traffic jams and long lines of cars. Our car overheated. There were about 100,000 people there, all anticipating another apparition.[6]

Van Hoof farm in Necedah

We had been told that if we looked at the sun at noon, when the Blessed Virgin Mary was supposed to appear, the sun would be spinning. Some people said they did see the sun spinning. Most didn't. Many people may have damaged their eyes. We left disappointed, like most other visitors, not really knowing whether there had been an apparition or not. But it was still a memorable experience.[7]

The Catholic Church investigated and said the visions were fake and never recognized that any miracle or wonder occurred there.

However, we did put Miracle Whip on our Wonder Bread sandwiches that day.

Mom was always deeply devoted to her Catholic faith. She hoped that Tom, Tony, or I might go into the priesthood. I never really thought much about becoming a priest, though. I did read about Saint William and decided that I wanted to become a saint like him instead.

I have certainly fallen far down in reaching my desire to become more saintly and a-better-version-of-myself. I still have much growing to do in that regard. Through good acts I am striving to achieve more Holy Moments, when I am the person God created me to be.[8]

Chapter 9: Mischief and Misadventures

One year I got a new hatchet for my birthday. That night I tried it out by chopping the legs off of an antique table in our basement. That was the only time I ever got a spanking at home.

When I was axed why I did it, I said that I had an axe to grind. I thought my Mommy would be upset with me, so I axed her if we could just bury the hatchet.

I also chopped down a lot of fruit bushes, because I wanted to hatchet the berry.

Often when I didn't get my way about something, I would hide in one of the hallway closets under a pile of clothes and listen to see if anyone knew where I was. Both of our hallway closets made great hiding places, although they were really dark and crowded with the stuff stored there. I came out of hiding when Daddy came home from work.

Sometimes when I was mad, I would climb up a tall old hickory tree by the back fence. I would stay up there most of the day, until I got hungry.

I always loved chocolate. I loved it so much, in fact, that sometimes when no one was looking, I would climb up on our kitchen counter, reach way up to the top shelf of the cabinet, take down one of Mom's baking chocolate bars, then run and find a good place to hide so I could secretly eat it. That baking chocolate tasted a little bitter, but that was OK—I knew I was getting away with something. Mom probably wondered what happened to all of her baking chocolate over the years.

I had to admit to getting into that chocolate, because I always believed that "Confection is good for the soul."

Baker's unsweetened chocolate

Many years later when I told Mom about eating the baking chocolate, she patted me on the knee and just said, "No, not my Billy!"

Our Aunt Kate used to baby-sit us sometimes, but she could be really grumpy and didn't want us in the kitchen when she was there. I remember she would sometimes shout at us, "You kids get out of the kitchen!"

We had another babysitter, Gertrude Snell. We called her Gert. She was the daughter of Naomi Snell, one of the ladies who did our laundry. When it was time to go to bed, we would sometimes crawl under our beds and hide from Gert.

We always tried to be on our pest behavior when we had a babysitter.

When Mom first gave me Heinz Baked Beans with the green label on the can, I absolutely loved them. They tasted so good that I immediately decided that I wanted to eat a whole can of them every day if possible. I took to climbing up on the kitchen counter when I was hungry; I would find a big can of those delicious Heinz Baked Beans on the top shelf, and secretly eat the whole can.

A Time of Innocence

My favorite beans

When I wanted to climb up on the counter, I said, "Bean me up, Scotty!" One day, though, Mom found out that the cans of baked beans were disappearing. I knew that I would have to spill the beans. I thought to myself, "To bean or not to bean." So I said to Mom, "I've bean thinking... most of the time I have bean a good boy, and what I did doesn't really amount to a hill of beans!" Mom thought I was full of beans, though.

When I went to confession at church, the priest told me that I would have to give up baked beans for Lentil I was sorry.

There was a problem, though, with eating too many beans. A study showed that if you eat beans continuously for six years and nine months, you produce the same amount of explosive gas as an atomic bomb. That is exactly why I tried to get a summer job working for the Atomic Energy Commission or the gas company.[9]

I also really loved to get into the icebox where Mommy kept a bottle of Phillips' Milk of Magnesia. It was mint-flavored, and it tasted so good that I would secretly drink a little every time I opened the icebox. Mommy apparently never noticed that the Milk of Magnesia was disappearing.

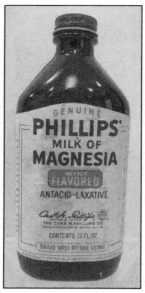

My favorite medicine

Today one of my favorite cocktails is Phillips' Milk of Magnesia, vodka, and orange juice. It's called a Phillips Screwdriver.

Chapter 10: Pranks and High Jinks

We ordered a lot of novelties, tricks, and pranks from the *Johnson Smith Catalog of Novelties*, such as itching powder, a radio mike, hot lips, a bending knife and fork, a fly on a spoon, a cut-off finger, a nail through the finger, a fake nail, a dribble glass, a trick guillotine, a vibrating hand shocker, a snapping pack of gum, garlic and hot chewing gum, midget cameras, and soap that turned black. We had great fun with everything we got from them.

Johnson Smith and Co. Novelties catalog

We also ordered a book from the *Johnson Smith Catalog* called *Art of Ventriloquism*. We practiced for hours trying to learn how to throw our voices. We wanted to be like the famous Edgar Bergen and his dummy, Charlie McCarthy.

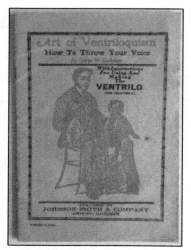

Ventriloquism book

We should have bought the book *Ventriloquism for Dummies.*
At one time, Tom, Tony, and I all had separate beds in the same small bedroom. We had green cowboy blankets on our beds and Cubs pennants on the walls. Tom and I each had twin-sized rollaway beds, while Tony slept on a chaise longue. Tom rigged up our clock radio and a record player to play the "The Yellow Rose of Texas" in the mornings to wake us up.

Chicago Cubs pennant that was above my bed

Tom and I loved to prank Tony, and he was always a good sport about it. Sometimes we rigged Tony's bed so that when he would lie down on it, the bed would collapse and poor Tony would unceremoniously slide off the bed onto the floor, a helpless victim of our latest prank!

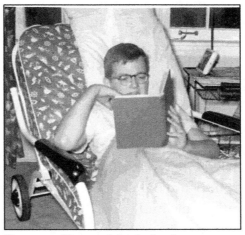

Tony reading on his chaise lounge

Did anyone ever find out who rigged Tony's bed?

Chef Boyardee apparently knew. Chef Boyardee was living all by himself in the big ziti and was feeling cannelloni. He was taking a walk just to pasta time away when a man named Mac elbowed his way through the crowd and said to him, "A penne for your thoughts." Chef Boyardee said, "I cannoli remember so much, and I cannot reveal my sauces, but I do know who rigatonis bed! They did it fusilli reasons, and I am going to shell the story to the National Enquirer."

Sometimes Tom and I would set the clock in our bedroom forward when we came home from dates or being out. We would then wake Tony and tell him it was time to get up for school. Tony would look at the clock, then jump out of bed and sleepily start getting dressed until he finally realized it was still dark outside and that he had been pranked. He would then go back to bed. Tony never seemed to get mad about it, though… he was such a great brother and good sport.

After going to bed, we sometimes liked to scare each other by quietly sneaking out of bed, very slowly creeping on the floor across the room in the dark, getting under one of our brothers' beds, and then suddenly pushing up on his mattress and shouting, "Wake up!"

Cream puffs were always my favorite pastry. There were two different bakeries that delivered pastries and bread to our house once a week. One was Stewart's Bakery, and the other was the Sunbeam Bakery.

Just for fun, we liked to hide behind the big forsythia bush at the edge of our driveway when the bakeries would deliver to our house. When the Sunbeam Bakery delivery truck would come, we would shout out, over and over, "Stewart's is better than Sunbeam!" Then when Stewart's came, we would of course yell repeatedly, "Sunbeam is better than Stewart's!"

I love puns about bread! So I thought I should stop loafing around and rise to the occasion before something goes a rye. The yeast I could do would be to write some good bread puns. I think I was born and bread a punster, and that puns must have been ingrained in me at an early age. I believe that bread puns are the best thing since sliced bread, and could make me the toast of the town, and might put me in the upper crust of society.

The Pillsbury Doughboy was my roll model. But he pasta way from a yeast infection and injuries from repeated pokes in the belly. Dozens of celebrities turned out to pay their respects, including Aunt Jemima, Mrs. Butterworth, Hungry Jack, Betty Crocker, Captain Crunch, and the California Raisins. The grave site was piled with many flours.

The Pillsbury Doughboy rose quickly in show business, but his life was filled with turnovers. He was a little flaky at times and was not considered a very smart cookie, but all he wanted was to be kneaded.

A Time of Innocence

He is survived by his wife Play Dough, and three children: John Dough, Jane Dough, and Dosey Dough (plus, they had one in the oven). He is also survived by his elderly father, Pop Tart.

I guess I'm on a roll here...

I know which side my bread is buttered on, so I think that if I could sell my bread puns, it would help me bake ends meet, and I could make a lot of dough, be a good breadwinner, and put bread on the table, as long as the puns were not stale or half-baked. I could charge everyone a pun-per-nickel, and if you could gluten of them together, they would make a long chain. Still, I know that man does not live by bread puns alone.

Zwieback in the day, nothing was butter than home-made bread. Just remember that everyone needs to stop and smell the flours, and if you want more bread puns, I am just a scone's throw away.

After reading all of these puns about bread, some people probably think I knead to have my bread examined!

Tom and I wanted to be able to tell when an intruder was standing in the hallway outside our bedroom door. We rigged up the register on the floor in front of the door so that when someone stepped on the register, a red light would flash on our desk console that Tom had made. We also glued an eyeball above our bedroom door so anyone standing there would think the eyeball was looking right down at them.

Tom and I also decided to put a two-way mirror on our bedroom door. We could see who was outside our door by peeking through the back of the mirror.

I thought at the time I might want to have a job cleaning mirrors someday, because I could see myself doing that.

Of course, in order to mount the two-way mirror, we had to cut a large hole in the door. Our parents didn't seem to mind too much. We also painted our bedroom door bright yellow.

In case someone might try to come into our room when we weren't there, we would sometimes set a booby trap by putting a cup of water on top of the door. When the door was opened, the cup of water would spill all over the unsuspecting intruder (usually one of my sisters).

One time when Susie's boyfriend, Kent Adams, came over to our house, Tom and I rigged up a radio in the living room so that we could talk into the radio from another room. We used a radio mike we had ordered from the *Johnson Smith Catalog of Novelties*.

When Kent came into our house, we announced over the radio, "We interrupt this program to bring you a special news bulletin just clearing our WRSW news desk. Kent Adam's house is on fire!"

Kent immediately ran outside, but Susie brought him right back in, and we then announced over the radio that if Kent Adams was listening, he was requested to "Bring his squirt gun to help fight the fire!" Susie stayed mad at Tom and me for a while after that.

Kent Adams

A Time of Innocence

We all liked Kent. He was a really nice guy and a star on the baseball, football, and basketball teams. Later we were sorry that we pulled such a mean prank.

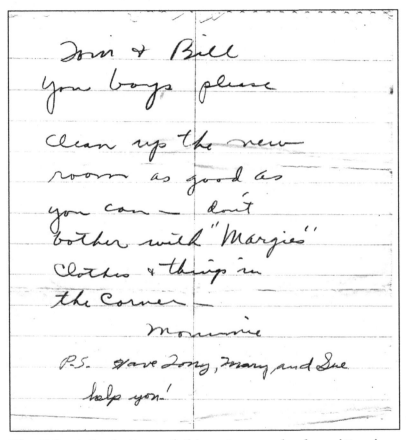

The P.S. at the bottom of this note was clearly written in a different handwriting—no doubt by Tom or me as yet another sibling prank.

Chapter 11: Getting Along Together

My brothers, sisters, and I were all close; most of the time we got along well and had fun playing together. I don't remember fighting with one another, except when we had boxing or wrestling matches. Mostly I played with Tom and Tony because they were the closest to me in age. We especially liked to play card games, board games, hide-and-seek, ping-pong, baseball, basketball, horseshoes, cops and robbers, and cowboys and Indians together.

Playing poker at the dining room table. (L-R) Susie, Tom, Margie, Tony, Mary Pat, and me

The worst name we ever called each other was "big dope." We also sometimes told each other to "shut up," although we knew we weren't supposed to say that. We never really said any other "bad" words. In fact, I don't think I even knew any swear words, and I don't remember ever hearing my parents, brothers, or sisters ever say any bad words, either.

A Time of Innocence

We had some funny nicknames for one another—Bill the Pill, Tom the Bomb, Tony the Bony, Mary Pat the Little Rat, Margaret Ellen the Watermelon, Sally Jo the Big Fat Toe, and Susan Jane Has No Brain. I'm not sure which one of us made these up, but I think it might have been me.

Sometimes we made written agreements about playing with one another.

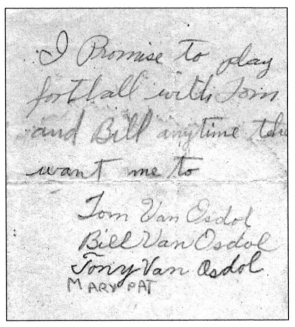

William R. Van Osdol, MD

Chapter 12: Indoor Games, Toys, and Activities

I loved to play cards and board games, especially on rainy days. My favorite card games were hearts (which Daddy taught us to play), rummy, and canasta.[10] I also liked to play Authors, Touring, tiddlywinks, and dominoes. My favorite board games were Monopoly, Cabby, Clue, and Go to the Head of the Class.[11]

My wonderful playthings included toy soldiers, western forts, Tinker toys, pick-up sticks, kaleidoscopes, wooden blocks, jacks, marbles, plastic bricks, Lincoln logs, a Lionel train set, puzzles, a Ferris wheel, a Li'l Abner band, doctor kits, hula hoops, yo-yos, coloring books (one of my favorites was *Tom Corbett Space Cadet*), a printing set, dart guns, a chemistry set, a wood-burning set, a Gilbert erector set, a Slinky, a View-Master, toy cars, tractors, trucks, and model airplanes.

Toy soldiers

Play doctor kit

Slinky

Li'l Abner band

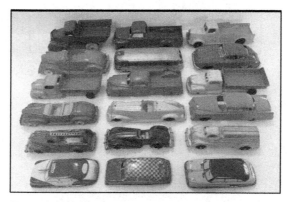

Toy cars

Dick Tracy car

Gene Autry and Hopalong Cassidy coloring books

Ferris wheel

Yo-yos

Lionel train set

Plastic bricks and Lincoln Logs

Coca-Cola truck

A Time of Innocence

Kaleidoscope, Tinker Toys and Pick-up Sticks

View-Master

We had some great dart gun fights in the back bedroom. Other games we played were musical chairs, hide-and-seek, and hide the thimble.

We also liked to play knights with our Prince Valiant swords and shields inside our home.

After all, a man's home is his castle — in a manor of speaking. Most people don't know this, but if the Knights of the Round Table had been late for their reservations at the restaurant, they would have been called the Knights of the Booth.

Sometimes we put on puppet shows. We also made walkie-talkies out of old tin cans and string.

William R. Van Osdol, MD

Chapter 13: Outdoor Games, Toys, and Activities

We spent hours every day in our woods playing soldiers, cops and robbers, hide-and-seek, and shooting our bows and arrows, Red Ryder BB guns, and slingshots. Tommy had a Wham-O slingshot, and we made other slingshots out of tree branches. We would go outside to play in the morning and sometimes would not come in until it was dark, except to eat.

Playing soldiers. Me and Tommy

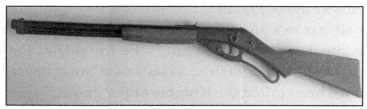

Red Ryder BB gun

A Time of Innocence

Wham-O slingshot

We had all kinds of play guns including army rifles, G-man guns, cap guns, cowboy guns, Buck Rogers and Space Cadet guns, pirate pistols, and squirt guns.

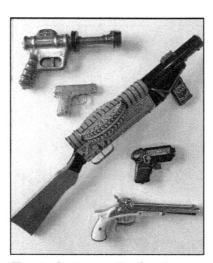

Top-to-bottom: Buck Rogers Atomic Pistol, detective gun, machine gun, G-man gun, and pirate pistol

We also liked to play cowboys and Indians in the woods. Hopalong Cassidy was always our favorite cowboy. Tommy, Tony, and I all had Hopalong Cassidy outfits, hats, and guns.

Hopalong Cassidy outfits. (L-R) Tommy, me, and Tony

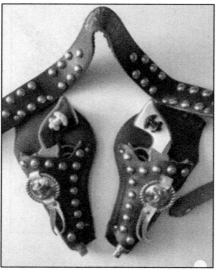

Hopalong Cassidy cap guns

A Time of Innocence

We liked other cowboys too, including Gene Autry, Roy Rogers, The Lone Ranger, Tom Mix, and Lash LaRue.[12]

Some of my favorite cowboy comic books. Top row: Lash Larue and Roy Rogers. Bottom row: Hopalong Cassidy and Gene Autry

We knew the names of most of their horses: Topper (Hopalong Cassidy), Champion (Gene Autry), Trigger (Roy Rogers), Silver (Lone Ranger), and Tony (Tom Mix).

Our favorite Indians were Straight Arrow and Tonto.

Straight Arrow target game

We didn't know then that Indians should be called Native Americans. We liked to pretend we were Tarzan when we played in the woods. Tommy thought we could find some vines to swing on.

Tarzan comic book

A Time of Innocence

But I thought, "That's another vine mess you'll get me in, Tommy!"

We also liked to wear our coonskin caps when we pretended to be Daniel Boone or Davy Crockett and made trails through the woods.

Davey Crockett coonskin cap

Other games we liked to play outside were kick the can, ring around the rosie, red rover, Simon says, fox and geese, leap frog, London Bridge is falling down, Mother may I, farmer in the dell, tug-of-war, Annie-Annie over, and blind man's bluff. We also made up a lot of our own games.

In the summer, we somehow found time to make ash trays out of clay (we quickly learned that they would break very easily), jump on pogo sticks, play tag, jump rope, catch lightning bugs, practice rope tricks, play on the swing set, ride our scooters, swing for hours in our hammocks, and have carnivals with games and prizes. We invited our cousins next door to come to our carnivals.

Once we practiced being trapeze artists on our swing set in the backyard, and then we put on a trapeze show when Daddy came home from work. When we put on the show, we sang, "He'd fly through the air with the greatest of ease, a daring young man on the flying trapeze!"

Tom, Tony, and I used to make little wooden paddle boats powered by rubber bands, which we would race from one side of the bridge to the other in the creek by Beyer's farm.

Tom, Tony, and I also all played—and loved—many different sports. Sally, Susie Jane, Mary Pat, and Margie were all very good athletes, and they played some of the sports with us, as well. They didn't have many organized sports for girls back then.

We played baseball, softball, basketball, ice hockey, flag and tackle football, wiffle ball, kickball, track and field (races, shot put, broad jump, high jump, and pole vaulting), horseshoes, volleyball, croquet, boxing, wrestling, badminton, archery, darts, and ping-pong on a table set up in the basement. We also liked to play with a boomerang.

At first we couldn't remember how to throw a boomerang, but then it came back to us.

We strung a net between two trees in the backyard, and we loved to play badminton there.

Once we had a puppy named Minton. He liked to chew on our shuttlecocks. Bad Minton!

We liked to shoot bows and arrows, most of which we made out of tree branches from our woods. Tommy even made a crossbow. We mostly shot our arrows just at bullseye targets.

Tommy liked archery better than I did. I thought archery had too many drawbacks. I was all a-quiver with excitement, though, when we shot our bows and arrows. Tommy and I had an archery match once and he beat me by an arrow margin.

I liked to pretend that I was William Tell when I practiced archery. He was a famous crossbow marksman who shot an arrow through an apple on his son's head. We never tried to shoot an apple off each other's head, but I think Tommy probably could have done it.

A Time of Innocence

William Tell comic book

Now I Will Tell you the rest of the story. William Tell and his son belonged to a bowling league. But historians have not been able to determine the name of the league's sponsors. So we'll never know for whom the Tells bowled.

William Tell was also a great cook. One day after preparing a new dish for his friends, he said, "I think there are one or two spices missing. What do you think?" Their answer was, "Only thyme, Will Tell!"

The William Tell Overture was the theme music for the radio show *The Lone Ranger.* I always remembered the show's introduction: "From out of the west — a fiery horse with the speed of light, a cloud of dust, and a hearty 'Hi-Yo Silver!' The Lone Ranger rides again!"

A friend once asked me, "Can I come overture house to listen to The Lone Ranger on the radio?" You could Tell he really liked the theme music.

The Lone Ranger comic book

I also liked to pretend sometimes that I was Robin Hood when I shot bows and arrows.
My favorite actor who played Robin Hood was Arrow Flynn.
Tom and I had some great boxing matches in our living room. We always wore boxing gloves, and you couldn't hit below the belt or above the chest. I liked to pretend that I was Rocky Marciano.

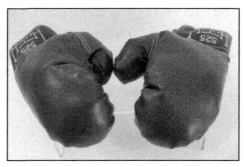

Our boxing gloves

A Time of Innocence

We also played a lot of croquet in our front yard.

When we played croquet, there was no rest for the wickets; we played with mallets toward none, because our reputation was at stake.

Behind the playhouse was a large sand and dirt pile where we would play with our trucks and cars for hours.

There was almost never any grass growing next to our house because of the bicycle races we had around the house. Mom and Daddy didn't seem to mind at all.

We dug pits next to the brown house so we could play horseshoes—one of our favorite outdoor games. We liked to say that "being close counts only in horseshoes and hand grenades."

We all wanted to compete in the Olympics someday, and to be just like Jim Thorpe, Jesse Owens, and Bob Mathias. Jim Thorpe, who was considered the greatest athlete of all time, won the pentathlon and decathlon in the Olympics. Jesse Owens won four gold medals and Bob Mathias won two.

Bob Mathias

Sometimes we held our own Olympic competitions. Our events included BB gun and pellet gun marksmanship, archery, the 100-yard dash, the shot put, the high jump, the pole vault, the javelin toss, and the broad jump. We used a heavy rock for the shot put and a long stick from the woods for javelin throwing. We made a sawdust pit for pole vaulting, high jumping, and broad jumping.

I wanted to run the 4-minute mile like Roger Bannister, who was the first person ever to do that.

We had big rocks that lined the semi-circular driveway in front of our house. It was great fun to try and walk all the way around this driveway while trying to step on every stone without falling off. One of my favorite stones lining the driveway was the one that looked like it had a deep imprint of a big toe.

When it was raining, we liked to sing, "It's raining, it's pouring, the old man is snoring!" When the rain stopped, we would go outside and splash barefoot in the big mud puddles that formed in the yard and driveway.

At night we liked to look up at the stars and find both the Big Dipper and the Little Dipper.

In the winter, we went sledding at Harry's Hole or down the big hill in the field behind our house. We also liked to ice skate and would play ice hockey at the pond in the corner of the field behind Munson's house, on Ford Lake, and on the backwaters of Pike Lake.

We built huge snow forts, had great snowball fights, and made tall snowmen. Even when it was bitter cold, we would bundle up and go outside to play.

A Time of Innocence

Ready to play ice hockey. (L-R) Me, Tom, and Tony

(L-R) Margie, Susie, Tom, Mary Pat, Tony, Sally, and me

Chapter 14: Adventures

One summer day, we found an abandoned car down the road next to our woods. That got us all excited. We thought it might be stolen, or that it could even belong to a gangster. It became a mystery that we called "The Case of the Abandoned Car." We worked on it for a while but never solved the case. Someone finally came and took the car away.

One night, we went camping in our small tent way back in the woods by our garden. But we forgot our matches, so we couldn't build a campfire. Tommy climbed high in a tree and began shouting as loud as he could, over and over, "Help! We forgot our matches! We forgot our matches!" Finally someone heard him and brought us a box of matches from home.

One day Tommy, Susan Jane, and I went camping in a tent next to the Tippecanoe River. There was a heavy rainstorm the first night. As we huddled together and listened to the loud rushing of the dark, swollen river and the constant battering of the rain on our little tent, we all became frightened that the river might overflow and wash us away. We couldn't call our parents to come and get us because there were no phones.

Although we didn't get much sleep, somehow we managed to make it through that night. By morning the rain had stopped so we walked into a little nearby town, Oswego, and bought ice cream cones. We went fishing on the river that day, and stayed another night without incident.

But to this day I still do not like to go camping.

Once I wanted to find out if my brothers and sisters liked camping, so I decided to take a pole. I found out that 100% of my brothers and sisters were unhappy when the tent collapsed. That was not my in-tent. Then the wind blew the tent away and we had a feeling we were not in canvas anymore. I have Toto recall about that event.

A Time of Innocence

One day in the freezing cold of winter, Tom and I were trying to clear an area to play ice hockey on the back waters of Pike Lake, way behind our house. Suddenly we both fell through the thin ice. We frantically managed to save ourselves, but we could easily have drowned. We had a frigid walk back home. I don't think our parents ever knew what a close call we had.

It would have been skating on thin ice to let our parents know what happened.

Tom, Tony, and I had a poster of Fredrick J. Tenuto hanging inside our closet door. He was a dangerous criminal known as the "Angel of Death" and was one of the FBI's 10 most wanted men. We always kept a lookout for Fredrick J. Tenuto because we wanted to help capture him.

Frederick J. Tenuto wanted poster (From the private collection of Eric T. Rebetti)

On weekends our parents sometimes took us to auctions on farms far out in the country. It was great fun going to those auctions, walking around looking at everything being auctioned off, and listening to the chants of the auctioneer.

The auctioneer's wife told us she had met him just by chants.

Our parents would buy a lot of things for our house at those auctions, and sometimes they would buy boxes of stuff for us for just a dollar, not knowing what was in the boxes. It was really exciting when we got home to go through those boxes and see what treasures were there. We would sometimes find old tools we could use.

One summer there was a report in the newspaper that someone had seen a leopard near Helser's farm, not far from our house. We thought the leopard must have escaped from somewhere. All that summer we watched out for it, scared that it might attack us.

I was so afraid that that I thought I might puma pants. Although they looked in several spots, no one ever spotted the leopard again. We called it "The Case of the Missing Lynx."

We had some small live turtles that we bought at the dime store in town. They came in different colors, and some had designs painted on their backs. Sometimes we had turtle races.

Live baby turtle. (Photo courtesy of Shine Gallery)

A Time of Innocence

We tried to find a rabbit to race our turtles, but then we decided that was a hare-brained idea.

When it was cold outside, we decided to shell-out the money to buy turtleneck sweaters for all of our little turtles.

One day one of our turtles crossed the street to go to the Shell station. We had to make it snappy to keep him from being hit by a car. That tortoise a lesson that we needed to watch the turtles better.

After that, the poor turtle was so upset that he was just a shell of his former self. However, he still liked to use his shell phone to take shellfies.

We were all fascinated by the stories Daddy would tell about a giant snapping turtle that had been sighted in a lake in the town of Churubusco, not far from Warsaw. The turtle was supposed to have weighed about 400 pounds and be as big as a dining room table! No one ever found the giant turtle, though, even when they drained the lake.

One of my dear friends now, Stan Schenher, grew up in Churubusco, but he never saw the famous turtle. Stan, who is also an avowed punster, is named after "Stan the Man" Musial, one of my favorite baseball players of all time.

One year Tommy, Tony, and I each got shiny new Columbia bicycles. We had great adventures riding those bikes. Sometimes we would ride into town to go to Fawley's or Schroeder's grocery stores, about a block apart on Fort Wayne Street. There we would buy old comic books, baseball cards, candy, drumsticks, and ice cream bars.

New bicycles. ((L-R) Tommy, me, and Tony

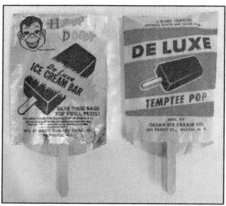

1950s ice cream bars

On lazy summer days, I also liked to swing in our front yard hammock and daydream. Summer seemed endless. As the song says, "Those were the days my friend, we thought they'd never end."[13]

We had a secret code we all knew just in case one of us might be kidnapped during one of our adventures. If any of us called on the phone, and the rest had any suspicion that the one calling was in trouble, we would say to him or her, "I found my green jacket today." (We all had nice green jackets that we liked to wear.) If the person calling was not in trouble or not being held by a kidnapper, he/she was supposed to respond by coughing into the phone, the secret code that everything was OK. But if the person calling said, "Oh, I'm glad you found your green jacket," or anything other than coughing, then we would immediately know that something was wrong and that we should call the FBI right away!

We made up a lot of written secret codes and would use them when we sent messages to each other.

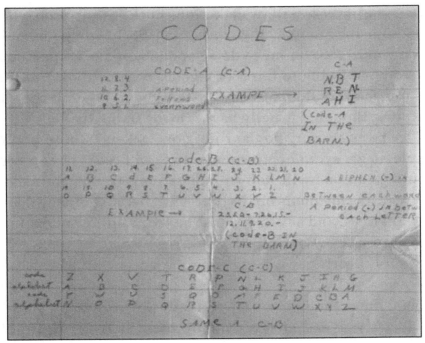

Secret codes

We also wrote secret invisible messages to one another using lemon juice. When we heated the paper with an iron, the writing turned brown and we could read the message.

Chapter 15: Chores

We had adventures every day, but we still needed to do all of our chores, which we gladly accepted. One job in the fall was to rake and burn all the leaves that had fallen in our yard. Because our woods had so many tall oak, maple, and shagbark hickory trees, we had mountains of leaves to rake. We would usually rake them into the woods.

If you are aspen for puns about trees, you are barking up the right tree. This may sound sappy, but I just love tree puns. I hope some of these willow make you chuck-le (knock on wood), and I hope they don't leaf you weeping. Still I wood knot mind if you would root for me to do a good job, because sometimes I get stumped trying to think of a good tree pun. Some of these tree puns are so old that I sawdust on them. When it comes to tree puns, though, I usually have it made in the shade.

Tree puns are very poplar right now, oak-ay? But sometimes people do get sycamore tree puns, and can't cedar reason why I should go on, so I will stop with these puns fir now, turn over a new leaf, log my hours on the time sheet because money doesn't grow on trees, and say to you, as the Jedi said, "May the forest be with yew!"

One of our chores was mowing the grass with a push hand mower.

Sometimes I fought the lawn and the lawn won.

Other chores included putting up the window screens in the spring and the storm windows before winter, and shoveling the steps and sidewalks in the wintertime.

One day Daddy asked me to wash and put up the window screens. It happened to be on a Sunday, so I said, "No, I can't do it, because God says you are not supposed to work on Sunday." (P.S.—I did not get in trouble for that.)

We also had to go down into the basement in the wintertime to shovel coal into the furnace. The coal was delivered by the coalman and was dumped down a chute into the coal bin.

We shoveled coal Night and Day like a Coal Porter.

The basement was dark and shadowy, and smelled of coal dust. When I was young, I was afraid to go down there by myself. I imagined the bogeyman could be hiding in the dark behind the furnace. So when I finished shoveling coal into the furnace, before running back up the stairs, I would repeat loudly, "I'll be back later, I'll be back later!" My thinking was that if the bogeyman <u>was</u> hiding down there, he might let me go upstairs if he knew I was coming back.

The black coal dust in our basement just didn't soot me. I could make even more puns about our basement, but that would be beneath me.

Since we didn't have any trash pickup back then, we carried out the trash and burned it at the back of our woods. Sometimes on windy days we had some really bad grass fires. We had to put them out with our water hoses. More than once, we even had to call the fire department to put out the fires.

Chapter 16: Baseball, Hot Dogs, Apple Pie, and Chevrolets

I grew up loving baseball, hot dogs, apple pie, and Chevrolets.

Baseball always seemed to be a part of me. I loved all the sights and sounds of baseball, including the ceremonious singing of our national anthem, the umpires shouting, "Let's play ball!" and "Strike three, you're out!", the cracks of the bats, the pops of the catchers' mitts, the roars of the crowd, the vendors yelling, "Get your hot dogs here!" and "Peanuts and Cracker Jacks!", the time-honored seventh-inning stretch, and the jubilant singing of "Take Me Out to the Ballgame."

(L-R) Daddy, me, Tom, and Tony

We had a baseball diamond in the back yard next to the woods. There was a wooden snow fence for a backstop, to keep the balls out of the woods. We still lost a lot of baseballs and softballs in the woods because the fence was not very high. We played baseball and softball in our front yard, as well. We often used the trees for bases when we played there.

One of our favorite games was one we called "wheelbarrow baseball." We played it on the side of the house, next to the crabapple tree and our little swimming pool. One of us would bounce a rubber ball off the inside of our wheelbarrow as hard as possible, and the "batter" would run the bases while the outfielder fielded the ball. We chose sides for teams, had bases (the crabapple tree was third base), and had a little wire home run fence at the edge of the woods.

Later, we started playing wiffle ball in the corner of the front yard by the street. I liked to pretend that I was Willie Mays or Mickey Mantle. That was our favorite game for a long time; we would play until it was so dark we could no longer see the ball.

1950s Wiffle Ball

We each looked forward to turning six years old. That was when Daddy would take us to Chicago on the train to see a Chicago Cubs baseball game (although Mary Pat and Margie, my younger sisters, never got to go, as I recall).

That Chicago trip was my very first train ride—and I was beyond excited! As I was standing on the crowded old Pennsylvania Railroad Depot platform in Warsaw, holding tightly to Daddy's hand, I could feel the vibrations of the tracks as the train approached. Then I heard the whistling, screeching, and thunderous noise as the diesel-powered train slowly rumbled into the station. The train was dark red with a yellow stripe. After it stopped and some passengers got off, the conductor yelled, "All aboard!" I slowly climbed up the steep steps with Daddy to board the railroad car and eagerly ran to find a seat next to a window.

Pennsylvania Railway train, the "Admiral", which we rode to Chicago. (Photo courtesy of American Railways)

As the train started up again and left the station, I listened to the chugging of the engine and the steady clickety-clack of the wheels. I looked out the windows in awe at the wondrous sight of all the small towns and fields as the train traveled from our little town of Warsaw to the big city of Chicago. I couldn't wait to get there.

Arriving in downtown Chicago, we excitedly got off the train at Union Station—a grand, historic, and ornate building with old wooden benches inside. It reverberated with the echoes of scurrying passengers.

A Time of Innocence

Union Railway Station in Chicago

I had never eaten peanuts before, and I wanted some to eat on the way to the game. So Daddy bought me a bag of peanuts in the shell from one of the vendors at the train station.

There was a long line of Checker and Yellow taxicabs parked right outside the train station. We climbed into one of the cabs to head out to Wrigley Field.

1940s Chicago Checker Taxi

After we got into the cab, I began eating the peanuts. I was in the back seat of the taxi, and Daddy was in the front. I started to complain, "Hey, Daddy, these peanuts don't taste very good!"

Daddy turned around and watched me for a second, then smiled and said in his usual kindly way, "Billy, you aren't supposed to eat the shells."

I was a little shell-shocked by the whole experience. I thought that the peanuts were just not all they were cracked up to be, and that's my story in a nutshell.

It was like a dream come true when I saw beautiful Wrigley Field for the very first time. I recognized the nearby streets, because I had heard the Cubs' radio announcers talk about Clark and Addison Streets, Sheffield Avenue, and Waveland Avenue (where home runs would sometimes land).

Wrigley Field in Chicago in the 1940s

I held on to Daddy as tightly as I could with one hand, while wearing my cherished baseball mitt on my other hand. We slowly entered Wrigley Field with the large crowd swelling and pushing all around us. After Daddy bought a Cubs yearbook, score-card, and pencil for each of us, we all ran excitedly up the ramp to find our seats in the stands.

A Time of Innocence

Chicago Cubs scorecard and yearbook

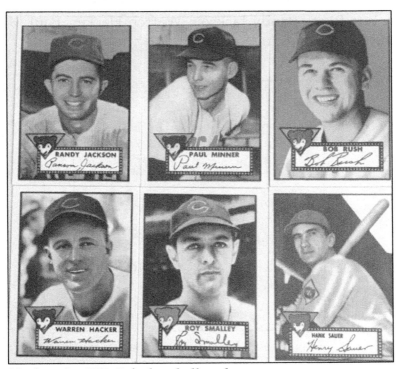

My favorite 1952 Cubs baseball cards

Then I saw the playing field for the very first time. It was such a thrill to see the towering grandstands, the plush green grass, the ivy-covered walls, and the Cubs players in their awesome white home uniforms and blue caps with red logos. The players were warming up on the field. I knew the names of all the Cubs, having collected all of their baseball cards, and I idolized each and every one of them.

Before the ballgame started, while the players were still warming up, I went down to the field beside the third base dugout and began asking the players for their autographs. The Cubs players were very friendly and willing to sign autographs. I got as many signatures as I could before the game started. All the Cubs players were my heroes; I kept and cherished every autograph that I could get from those players, including Hank Sauer, Bob Rush, Randy Jackson, Warren Hacker, Paul Minner, Phil Cavarretta, and Roy Smalley.[14]

Autographed 1948 Cubs baseball

I did keep score during that first game, but I really don't remember who won. While I didn't catch any foul balls, it didn't matter, because I had the time of my life that day!

Even though the Cubs almost never had a winning season and were often in last place, I always remained a loyal, steadfast Cubs fan throughout my childhood. Wrigley Field was like hallowed ground to me.

You might call this grandstanding, but I think there are about 1-2 million baseball fields in the world. That's just a ballpark figure. To estimate the number of fields you need a baseline, and I may be way out in left field with this guess.

There must have been baseball fields around since Adam and Eve, because the Bible says, "In the big inning, God made Heaven and Earth."

I wore my Cubs baseball cap most of the time after that. I even wore it to bed.

1957 Chicago Cubs cap

That may be the reason I don't have much hair on my head today. This may be neither hair nor there, but when I was combing through the newspaper ads, I found a very nice, expensive men's hairpiece. I didn't buy it though, because I thought it was way too much toupee. I still carry my old comb — I just can't part with it.

I secretly always wanted to play for the Cubs when I grew up. My favorite Cubs player when I was younger was Hank Sauer. When I got older, it was "Mr. Cub," Ernie Banks.

1954 Ernie Banks rookie card

Some of my favorite baseball players on other teams included Joe DiMaggio, Mickey Mantle, Hank Aaron, Yogi Berra, Willie Mays, Ted Williams, Duke Snider, Al Kaline, Warren Spahn, and Stan Musial.[15]

Joe DiMaggio

A Time of Innocence

My favorite baseball cards. (L-R) Top row: Ted Williams, Al Kaline, and Hank Aaron. Middle row: Yogi Berra, Willie Mays, and Mickey Mantle. Bottom row: Warren Spahn, Stan Musial, and Duke Snider

I idolized famous Baseball Hall of Fame players such as Babe Ruth, Lou Gehrig, Ty Cobb, Honus Wagner, Rogers Hornsby, Dizzy Dean, and Christy Mathewson.[16]

I also liked the Indianapolis Indians. One of my prized possessions was a certificate for one share of stock in that baseball team.

William R. Van Osdol, MD

Indianapolis Indians stock certificate from 1955

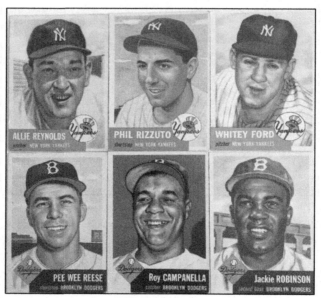

Yankees and Dodgers 1953 baseball cards

In those days, it was usually the Brooklyn Dodgers and the New York Yankees who played in the World Series. My favorite players on the Dodgers were Duke Snider, Roy Campanella, PeeWee Reese, Jackie Robinson, Gil Hodges, Carl Furillo, and Sandy Koufax. My favorite Yankees were Mickey Mantle, Phil

A Time of Innocence

Rizzuto, Yogi Berra, Allie Reynolds, Vic Raschi, Whitey Ford, and Billy Martin.

Baseball was so popular at that time that our teachers would sometimes let us listen to the World Series in our classrooms.

We were all extremely excited when Little League baseball came to Warsaw. One of the most memorable days of my childhood was when I got to try on my first Little League baseball uniform. Tommy and I were on the same Cubs Little League team that first year, and the next year Tony was also on the Cubs team.

(L-R) Tom, me, Margie, Mary Pat, and Tony

The Cubs manager was Lewis "Peanuts" Breading, the owner of Breading's Cigar Store. The assistant manager was Kent Adams, who would become Susie's boyfriend.

Little League baseball was so popular in Warsaw that local radio personality Bill Long announced the games over WRSW radio. Every game was written up, including box scores, in the Times-Union, Warsaw's newspaper.

Our Cubs team won the Little League championship that first year in 1952. Some of my friends on the first Little League Cubs team were Don Pittenger, Jon Swoverland, John Foresman, and Bob Phillips.[17]

Some friends on other teams were Eddie Huffer and Dave Delp on the Cardinals, and Jim Aker and Steve Parsons on the Yankees.

One year when I was trying out for the Little League All-Star team, they hit me a fly ball during fielding practice. I apparently couldn't see the ball, or maybe just misjudged it, and the ball bounced right off the top of my head.

I wondered why the ball kept getting bigger and bigger . . . and then it hit me. . . .

When I was a little older, I got talked into umpiring my first Little League game when one of the umpires didn't show up. There was a very close play at second base when the runner slid in, and I quickly shouted "Safe!" while making the signal for safe with my hands.

Suddenly most of the crowd in the stands stood up and with a loud roar began screaming and yelling at me, shouting that I must be blind, and that the runner was out! So not knowing exactly what I should do—it was, after all, the first game I had ever umpired—I decided that I should just change the call. So I yelled, "No, he's out!" while making the signal for out with my thumb in the air. Immediately the <u>rest</u> of the crowd went wild. They didn't ask me to umpire any more.

I played right field and Tom played center field on one of our teams. I never had to worry when I missed a ball or it went through my legs, because Tom was usually there to back me up. Tom knew that I wasn't always the greatest fielder, and he fielded the ball himself if I missed it.

A Time of Innocence

When I was older, I also played Pony League and American Legion baseball.

Pony League

After the ball games, I liked to go to the concession stand and buy banana Turkish taffy. I also always looked forward to ice cold soda after the games. My favorites were Pepsi, RC Cola, and Nehi. My favorite flavors of Nehi were cream soda, strawberry, and grape.

William R. Van Osdol, MD

My favorite sodas

We always had soda pop on the Fourth of July because, although it may sound corny, it should always be, "Nehi by the Fourth of July." *(Midwesterners will understand...)*

I loved to eat hot dogs with a soda when attending baseball games. Hot dogs always seemed to taste so much better at a ball game than anywhere else.

As it happens, Babe Ruth also loved hot dogs. He once ate 24 of them between games of a doubleheader. One time he ate so many hot dogs at a ballgame that he had to be taken to the hospital.

Mom and Mamaw made the best pies ever. Apple pie was always one of my favorites. We sometimes had pie-eating contests in our backyard when we had family reunions. We would all sit at a table with our hands behind our backs and try to eat the pies—apple, raspberry, or blackberry—using only our mouths. The winner was the one who ate the most pie in one minute.

We had a rhubarb patch in our garden, so another one of our favorites in the contest was rhubarb pie.

A Time of Innocence

I remember, too, that we had some rhubarbs about who was the winner of those pie-eating contests.

Babe Ruth wouldn't be outdone when it came to eating pies, either. He once ate 12 pies between games of a doubleheader.

I tried baking a pie myself once, but Betty Crocker came and threw rocks at our windows.

We also had watermelon seed spitting contests in our backyard when we had family reunions. (The record for the farthest watermelon seed spitting is 75 feet and 2 inches.)

I wouldn't believe it if I hadn't seed it with my own eyes!

Chevrolets were always a part of our life, too. Daddy would buy a shiny new Chevrolet station wagon about every three or four years. One of our first station wagons was a green Woodie. Later we had a 1956 silver and white Chevy station wagon—that was my favorite. I learned to drive in a blue 1959 Chevy station wagon.

1950 Chevrolet Woody station wagon. Inside (L-R) Tommy, Tony, Sally Jo, Mary Pat, and me

1956 Chevrolet station wagon. Inside (L-R) Margie, Mary Pat, and Tony

1959 Chevrolet station wagon

It was always an exciting time for us when Daddy drove a new station wagon home and we all piled in to go for a ride. Daddy bought the new cars from Munson's Chevrolet; the Munsons were our cousins and next door neighbors, and their kids—Elaine and Dee—sometimes came over to play with us.

Chapter 17: Basketball

I always had a passion for basketball. I loved hearing the rhythmic dribbling of the ball on the hardwood court, the squeak of tennis shoes, the shrill whistles of the referees, the sweet swish of the ball going through the net, and the cheers of the crowd.

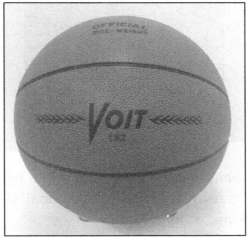

1950s Voit basketball

We used to put basketball rims made of clothes hangers above the inside of our front door and play basketball in the living room. It just about ruined the top of the front door (and we just <u>may</u> have knocked over a few lamps during games…). Our parents never seemed to mind much.

When playing basketball in the living room, I liked to pretend that I was Whitey Bell, Warsaw's most famous basketball player and my hero. He was the first Warsaw player to score more than 1,000 points, and he was also the star quarterback on the football team. Whitey Bell went on to play basketball for North Carolina State and the New York Knickerbockers.

William R. Van Osdol, MD

Whitey Bell

Sometimes when shooting baskets, I would pretend that I was one of the other Warsaw High School basketball stars, such as Sam Joyner, Kent Adams, or John McCoy.

We were thrilled when Daddy had a cement basketball court built in our backyard. We spent many hours on that court practicing, as well as playing one-on-one, horse, and twenty-one.

I was always very excited when Daddy would watch me practice basketball through the dining room window, always hoping that he would see me make some long shots.

I also liked to pretend that I was Bobby Plump, the player who made the winning basket for little Milan High School with three seconds left to beat mighty Muncie Central in 1954 and win the state basketball championship. (*By the way, that was the game that was celebrated in the famous movie "Hoosiers", starring Gene Hackman.*)

Bobby Plump was named "Mr. Basketball" by the Indianapolis Star newspaper and received the coveted Trester Award for

Mental Attitude that year. I always dreamed of winning the Trester Award, too.

Bobby Plump

Bobby Plump now owns a restaurant in Broad Ripple (near Indianapolis) called "Plump's Last Shot."

I spent many hours playing basketball at the Baker's Boys Club, which was in the gymnasium at the high school. It was run by our beloved Coach Pete Thorn. Coach Thorn had been a legendary athlete at Wabash College, where he was awarded 16 letters for basketball, football, baseball, and track.[18]

My favorite college basketball players were Don Schlundt, Jimmy Rayl, Tom Bolyard, Bobby Leonard, Joe Sexson, Mel Garland, and Terry Dischinger.

My favorite professional basketball team was the Fort Wayne Zollner Pistons, and my favorite players on that team were George Yardley, Larry Faust, and Mel Hutchins.

Pistons program

George Yardley

Other professional basketball players I liked. Top row: Oscar Robertson and George Mikan Bottom row: Bob Cousy and Wilt Chamberlain[19]

Chapter 18: Football

We liked to play flag, touch, or tackle football in our back yard. We sometimes had friends come over just to play. I got the wind knocked out of me many times after being tackled, and that was always a scary feeling.

1940s football

When he played football his freshman year, my brother Tom would practice kicking field goals in our backyard.

Some of my favorite professional football players were Otto Graham, Elroy "Crazylegs" Hirsh, Johnny Unitas, Sammy Baugh, and Bobby Layne. My favorite football players from earlier times were Bronco Nagurski, Red Grange ("The Galloping Ghost"), and Jim Thorpe.[20]

I liked to listen to Notre Dame football games on the radio on Saturdays. My favorite Notre Dame players were Ralph Guglielmi, Johnny Lattner, Joe Heap, Neil Worden, Johnny Lujack, and Paul Hornung.[21]

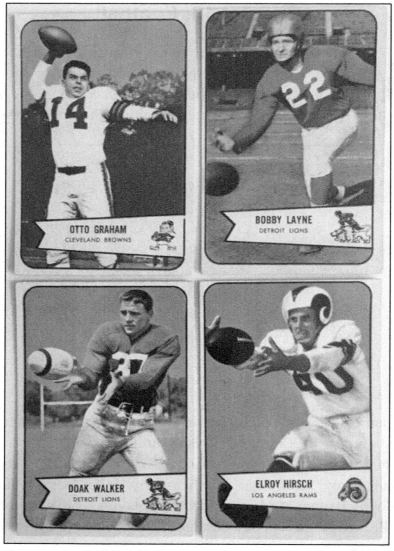

Favorite football cards. Top row: Otto Graham and Bobby Layne. Bottom row: Doak Walker and Elroy Hirsch

A Time of Innocence

Notre Dame football players. (L-R) Johnny Lujack, Paul Hornung, and Ralph Guglielmi

My favorite Notre Dame football coaches of all time were Knute Rockne, Frank Leahy, and Terry Brennan.

Knute Rockne football card

Daddy would sometimes take us to Notre Dame football games in South Bend. He used to say to us, "Never bet against Notre Dame or the Yankees."

Notre Dame football stadium

1950s Notre Dame football tickets

Nothing was more thrilling to me than when the Notre Dame band marched onto the field playing the "Notre Dame Victory March."

A Time of Innocence

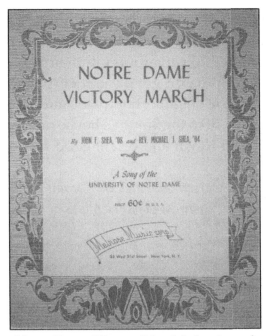

"Notre Dame Victory March" sheet music

I came to love Notre Dame over the years, and it was really a dream come true for me when I was able to attend college there.

Notre Dame Administration Building

Sometimes we would go over to the Huffers' house on Detroit Street to play flag football with Billy and Eddie, two of our best friends. We also liked to run around in their foundry and throw clods at each other. When it got dark, their parents would show movies outside for the neighborhood kids and us.

We sometimes went to the Smyth's house on East Market Street to play football with Kevin and Brian, good friends who went to our church.

Later, Kevin and I were roommates in Keenan Hall our first year at Notre Dame. We have remained good friends ever since.

Chapter 19: Golf and Tennis

Although I never played golf, my favorite professional golfers were Ben Hogan, Sam Snead, and Arnold Palmer.[22] (I did like to play miniature golf, however.)

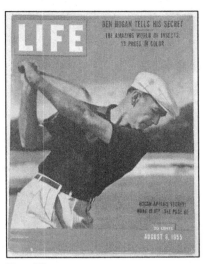

Ben Hogan

After we went to church on Sunday, Daddy would often take us to the B & K Root Beer stand across from the Flagpole for the greatest root beer floats ever.

Sometimes he would drive us up to North Webster to play miniature golf. On the way, we would always stop to get a drink of water from the flowing well by the side of the road. We took our baseball bats with us so that we could also go to the batting cage that was right next to the miniature golf course.

A fairway to roughly putt it is that the miniature there, you could see that it was almost impossible fore you to get a hole-in-one, and that would really tee us off. We would still take an extra pair of socks in case we got a hole in one, but, darn, we never did. I hope these golf puns are par for the course.

B & K Root Beer stand. (Photo courtesy of Michelle J. Bormet, *A History of the City of Warsaw, Indiana*)

Flowing well. (Photo courtesy of Indiana Album)

I liked to play tennis, although I didn't play too much when I was younger. My favorite tennis players were Pancho Gonzales, Jack Kramer, and Tony Trabert.[23]

A Time of Innocence

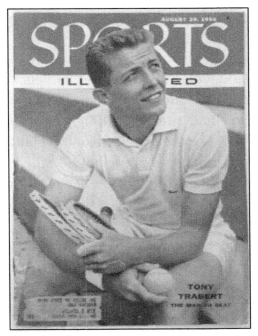

Tony Trabert

A girl named Annette, standing in the center of the tennis court, decided she wanted to date a tennis player. Her approach was to search the net where she found the perfect match. Her first date with the tennis player was set around tennish in the morning at Denny's, where they were served a Grand Slam. Then they decided to go dancing at a Tennis Ball, where they had too much to drink, got smashed, made a loud racquet, and were out of line. It wasn't her fault that she didn't know this be forehand (before he courted her), but love means nothing to tennis players. Some tennis players also like to give you backhanded compliments or string you along, and some can be self-serving.

Here is some good advice—invest in tennis balls because they have a high rate of return.

William R. Van Osdol, MD

Chapter 20: Young Writers

One year Tom and I wrote some adventure books by hand on yellow Goldenrod tablets. We both wrote stories about the Craig Boys, John and Ted, and their friend Chet, who "had many thrilling adventures and solved exciting mysteries." They were a lot like the Hardy Boys.

Tom wrote one Craig Boys book that he called, *The Mark on the Knife*; I wrote one entitled *The Mystery of Gull Island*.

Tom also wrote a book about *The Van Osdol's Adventures* that he called *The Mystery of the Old Cellar*. It was a story he made up about a gang of bank robbers. Tommy, Billy, and Tony found the robbers hiding in a shack the robbers had built over the old cellar near Ford Lake and Dalton's Lane. They had a shoot-out with the robbers at the white barn down the road from their house. They used their air rifles, BB guns, and bows and arrows to capture the robbers. At the end of the story, they got a nice reward that they put in the bank, to go to college and buy a car.

```
THE VAN OSDOL'S
   ADVENTURES

   THE MYSTERY OF THE
       OLD CELLAR

   WRITTEN BY:
       TOM VAN OSDOL

   ILLUSTRATED BY:
       TOM VAN OSDOL


   DEDICATED TO:  VAN OSDOL FAMILY


COPYRIGHT
  1955
                    Started: Dec 30, 1954
                    Finished: Jan. 1, 1955
```

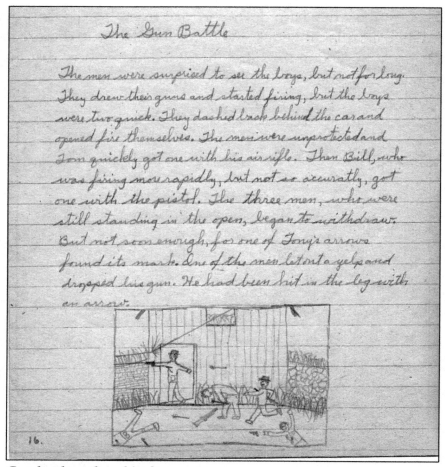

Gun battle at the white barn

One day I decided to start writing numbers in my yellow notebook, beginning with the number one, to see how long it would take me to write to a million. I didn't get very far before I gave up.

After getting a printing set one Christmas, we started printing a family newspaper. We wrote mostly about family news, but the paper also included a sports section, a comic strip, and jokes. We called the paper the Family Tribune and sold it for two cents.

A Time of Innocence

Family newspaper

It seems we were once again following in our Daddy's footsteps. He studied journalism at DePauw University, and before going to dental school he worked as a sports writer at the *Indianapolis Star*.

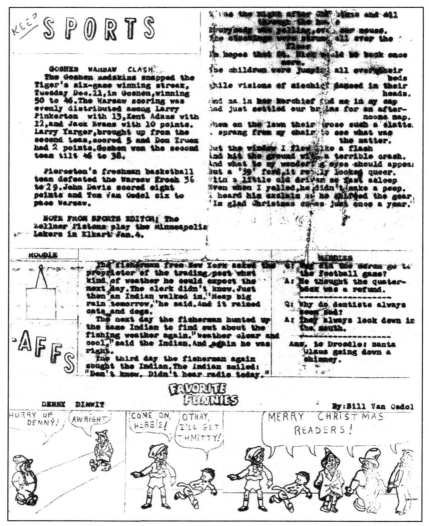

Family newspaper

Tom and I also wrote several radio scripts to broadcast through our radios, using the radio mike that we had ordered from the *Johnson Smith Catalog of Novelties* (see Appendix A).

A Time of Innocence

News Broadcast

This is station WKJQ, coming to you from Fort Worth, Texas. Time now, ——. Stay tuned for the news every hour on the hour with Jack Gearheart as your news commentator. Office. Hello Ladies and Gentlemen. This is your happy news commentator Jack Gearheart and here we go, into the news. In Russia: 16 captured airmen have been brutally murdered as they marched, on what they thought, was a march to freedom across the border. (What Oh, thank you.) Ladies and gentlemen. It has happend. The earth is being invaded by space ships from outer space. They have landed in Indiana near Gary, and are moving Southeast, destroying everything in their path. The following cities are asked to be on guard against an attack. Plymouth, Warsaw, Col. City, Ft. Wayne, and any other towns included in this area. The creatures from these space ship seem to be like mechanical men, or robots, operated by some other civilization from elsewhere besides earth. The creatures are seemingly unstoppable. If you should happen to see one, do not try to fight it, run. (rattle paper)

Here's another special bulletin. The president has just called a national emergency meeting. The army and air force can not seem to be able to destroy them, even with their modern war equipment. Please stand by. All programs scheduled for this broadcast are cancelled. This station will be used only to broadcast only news and warnings of this national disaster.

Chapter 21: Dogs

Our first dog was a full-blooded collie; her registered name was Bonnie Colleen of Loadstone. We called her just "Bonnie." Sadly she got run over by a car when she was not very old.

(L-R) Bonnie, Tommy, Tony, Sally Jo (in back), me (in front), and Susan Jane

Nellie was our next dog, and we all loved her. Sometimes she would come home smelling terrible after running around in the fields and creeks all day. If she was sleeping under the dining room table and we hadn't given her a bath yet, we would say, "Nellie, you stink!"—and she would get up and walk slowly out of the room.

A Time of Innocence

Nellie

We should have let a sleeping dog lie.

Unfortunately, Nellie had to have one of her legs removed after she caught it in a fence.

Nellie always seemed to be having puppies. We usually kept the puppies in the brown house when they were little. We drew numbers out of a hat to choose which puppies would be ours.

Once, when we were drawing numbers out of a hat, I drew 6 ⅞.

If you are wanting puns about dogs, you are barking pup the right tree. Nellie reminded me of the three-legged dog who walked into the bar in the old West and said, "I'm looking for the man who shot my paw!"

Once I couldn't think of a name for my puppy. My brothers hounded and dogged me to come up with one. I knew it was about time I did, so I thought about naming my puppy Timex or Rolex, but that was only because I wanted a watchdog.

I finally decided to name that puppy Achilles. When I tried to train him, I said, "Achilles, heel," but he never learned to do it. I guess that was his weakness.

One year Nellie had her puppies out by the road, which was litterally just asking fur trouble, because the police came by and tried to make a collar, and they gave her a ticket fur littering.

Nellie always kept warm in the winter. She had not only a nice fur coat, but also pants.

Once we threw a stick five miles away, and, doggone, Nellie still retrieved it. You might think that is far-fetched. She did work her tail off, and worked like a dog to find the stick. She was dog-tired and a little hot under the collar when she got home, but she went right to sleep in her pup tent.

We wanted to send her to obedience school to work on her dogtorate degree, but we couldn't get her in because of her low S.I.T. scores.

Nellie liked to go almost everywhere with us, but for some reason she refused to go to the Flea Market. She just wanted to stay in the barking lot.

It was ruff being a dog, and Nellie was sic as a dog sometimes, especially in the dog days of summer, but her Labs were usually OK. Once her canines were bothering her, and we thought the leash we could do was to take her to a dentist. When we took her to the vet because her eyes were red, the vet said, "Whoa, Nellie! You are a sight fur sore eyes!"

Nellie liked to eat hush puppies very quietly, but her favorite food was hot dogs, because it's a dog-eat-dog world. Nellie liked to bark a lot, but I Noah another dog who didn't ark at all. Nellie also liked to eat watermelons, especially when she was feeling down and a little melon collie.

You might think that you can't teach an old dog new tricks, but Nellie learned to push paws on the TV set, and her favorite shows were the Adventures of Sherlock Bones and anything written by Bark Twain. She liked to eat pupcorn when she watched TV. Her favorite talk show host was Bob Barker.

Nellie tried to play classical music on our piano, but her Bach was worse than her bite.

Sometimes Nellie would bring me toilet paper when I was in the bathroom. She thought she was a lavatory retriever.

A Time of Innocence

Believe it or not, Nellie also learned how to play poker. But she was not a very good gambler, because every time she got a good hand, she wagged her tail!

We adopted another dog once that had belonged to a blacksmith. We knew that because as soon as we got him home, he made a bolt for the door.

I am going to stop here—I don't want you to be roverdosed on dog puns.

Our last dog was a little black and brown toy fox terrier named Pudgy. She was really Mary Pat's dog; sadly, she also got run over by a car.

Margie, Mary Pat, and Pudgy

William R. Van Osdol, MD

hapter 22: Candy, Gum, Cracker Jacks, and Ice Cream

My favorite candy included Baby Ruth, Turkish Taffy, Sky Bar, and candy cigarettes.[24] The candy cigarettes said "Just like Dad!" on the display box.

Candy display including Sky Bar and Necco wafers

Candy cigarettes

A Time of Innocence

I loved chewing gum; my favorites were Black Jack, Clove, and Beemans. My favorite bubble gums were Bazooka, Dubble Bubble, and the gum from packs of baseball cards.[25]

Chewing gum and bubble gum

"I haven't had any tooth decay yet," I once told Daddy precariously.

I did get a lot of cavities from chewing so much bubble gum, and Daddy had to fill them at his office. One time when I had an appointment to fill some cavities and I was feeling brave, I said, "Daddy, I don't want you to numb me with novocaine, because I don't like getting shot with that needle." Daddy tried to talk me out of it, but I wouldn't change my mind. So he starting drilling without novocaine. Well, I didn't last very long. That pain was so bad! Of course, Daddy then had to go ahead and give me novocaine, that day, and every time after that.

I should have taken the shot to begin with, because I knew the drill. Later on, though, for being one of his best patients, I got a little plaque as an award.

I liked Cracker Jacks, mostly because of the great prizes that were in every box, including colorful plastic figures of cowboys,

Indians, baseball players, clowns, policemen, bears, and other things.

Cracker Jacks prizes

Animal crackers, which came in Barnum's Animals boxes or cardboard bus boxes, were my favorite cookies.

Animal Crackers box

I always loved ice cream. We could have it only on Sunday nights. Sealtest and Schlossers were my favorite brands. I also liked Dixie Cup ice cream. I collected the Dixie Cup lids, which had pictures of movie stars, cowboys, and baseball players.

Sealtest ice cream

Humphrey Bogart and Tom Mix Dixie Cup ice cream lids

One of our favorite things to do in the summertime was to make homemade ice cream. Mom had the best recipe to make vanilla ice cream (see Appendix B).

We had to take turns turning the handle of the ice cream maker, because it became really hard to crank after a while. When the ice cream was finally made, we thought it was the greatest treat in the world.

We were all probably a little cranky after making the ice cream.

Chapter 23: Souvenirs, Novelties, and Pop

We loved making scatter pins out of plaster of Paris and rubber molds that Daddy brought home from his dental office. We had rubber molds for Santa Claus, Christmas trees, wreaths, snowmen, fish, turtles, and dogs.[26]

Some scatter pins we made

We would all sit around the dining room table and work on the pins together. We spent hours painting them with water colors and putting coats of shellac on them.

We tried to sell the pins and soft drinks at a little stand in our front yard next to the street. When a car drove by, we shouted, "Souvenirs and novelties, ten cents! Ice cold pop, ten cents!"

We also had fun weaving different colored pot holders on little square peg looms. We sold them at our front yard stand, too.

(L-R) Margie and Mary Pat at stand in front yard

We didn't use wool on our looms, but I have herd that some weavers like sheep puns, so here ewe go...

I overherd that there was a little girl named Bo who lost some sheep and didn't know where to find them. But she didn't say a Peep about how the sheep got lost. The sheep had tumbled down a hill and it was a lambslide. There is mutton like a lambslide to cause shear terror, believe ewe me. I herd one of the sheep in the center of the flock singing "Stuck in the Middle with Ewe." People flocked to the hill to see what happened, although some of them felt a little sheepish for doing so.

Just between ewe and me, the sheep should have made a ewe-turn, but maybe someone was trying to pull the wool over their eyes. Or maybe the black sheep of the family was trying to fleece them, or there was a wolf in sheep's clothing there. But accidents wool happen, and whatever wool be, wool be. Maybe they just wanted to get some sheep thrills.

They had to rent a Ewe-Haul to get the sheep back up the hill. It was not easy, but where there's a wool, there's a way. If ewe want, you can watch all of this on EweTube.

I have a Dicken's of a time resisting telling you this, but at Christmas time, when there is fleece on earth and good wool to men, I herd that when some sheep go, "Baaah!" other sheep reply, "Humbug!"

You may not like sheep puns, but there are several famous people besides me who do like them, including J.R. Eweing, Meryl Sheep, Lady BaBa, and Britney Shears. I am done with these puns now, so I am going to take it on the lamb and start counting sheep on my sheep number bed.

I know, some of these are really baaaad puns!

Chapter 24: Ballads, Poems, Plays, and Pantomimes

Uncle Jim (Robinson) often recited "The Ballad of Johnny Sands" at our family reunions. I asked him to send me a copy of it; I memorized the ballad and recited it sometimes at subsequent family get-togethers (see Appendix C).

I was just following in our Daddy's footsteps. Daddy used to recite a long poem for us called *The Charge of the Light Brigade*. We especially loved to hear him recite the line, "Into the valley of Death rode the six hundred."[27]

Another favorite poem Daddy liked to recite was *The Shooting of Dan McGrew*. The first line was, "A bunch of the boys were whooping it up in the Malamute saloon." It was about Dangerous Dan McGrew and "the lady that's known as Lou."[28]

We also loved it when Daddy would read us the poem *Little Orphant Annie*, by James Whitcomb Riley. We always remembered that "the goblins will get you if you don't watch out!"

James Whitcomb Riley book

On holidays, we sometimes put on plays for our family and relatives. One year we put on a Fourth of July play; at the end, we staged a firecracker explosion. We laid down on the floor with ketchup all over us, and one of us held a sign that said, "Be safe, not sorry."

It was the last show we put on, and we wanted to end with a bang, although in Heinz-sight, putting ketchup everywhere may not have been a good idea. Everyone knew I was the one who spread ketchup everywhere, because I was caught red-handed.

But as the Jedi said, "May the Fourth be with you!"

We put on pantomimes for our family of Stan Freberg's "St. George and the Dragonet" and "Little Blue Riding Hood." "St. George and the Dragonet" was a spoof of the radio program, *Dragnet*.

When we visited our Kiefer cousins in Elwood in 1953 to celebrate Uncle John and Aunt Sarah's 40th wedding anniversary, Mary Pat recited, "I Tawt I Taw a Puddy Tat."[29]

Mary Pat standing and reciting poem at Kiefer's home

Chapter 25: Family Vacations

Each year we looked forward with great anticipation to August, because Daddy usually took most of that month off from work to take us on vacation. We were so excited about going on vacation that we would start packing weeks ahead. We usually drove up to Michigan, where we formed many fond memories. As we were driving there, I was always the one who every few miles asked, "Are we there yet?"

We played many games in the car while on those trips, including twenty questions (animal, vegetable, or mineral), I spy, license plate game, the alphabet game (from signs), and my father owns a grocery store. We also played hangman and tic-tac-toe.

Our favorite songs to sing in the car were "Found a Peanut," "She'll Be Coming 'Round the Mountain," "Old MacDonald Had a Farm," and "Row, Row, Row Your Boat."

We liked reading the Burma-Shave signs along the sides of the highways. They were poems in a series of six funny rhyming signs, ending with "Burma-Shave."[30] One of my favorites was: "Around / The curve / Lickety-split / It's a beautiful car / Wasn't it? / Burma-Shave."[31]

In Michigan, we would usually go to either Pleasant Lake Lodge near Three Rivers or Wildwood Resort on Cedar Hedge Lake near the little town of Bendon. Once while on the way to Three Rivers, we stopped at the Chief White Pigeon Monument near White Pigeon, Michigan.

Speaking of pigeons, that reminds me that I was pigeon-toed when I was little. My doctor told me I had to wear orthopedic shoes. I didn't think they would help, but I stand corrected.

Chief White Pigeon monument. (L-R) Me, Tony, Tommy, Susie, Sally Jo, and Mary Pat

Pleasant Lake. (L-R) Me, Tony, Daddy, Tommy, Mary Pat, Susie, and Sally Jo

A Time of Innocence

We stayed in a cabin on Little Pleasant Lake when we went to the Pleasant Lake Lodge. Sometimes we would drive over to nearby Big Pleasant Lake and go swimming or fishing. One time while we were swimming there, we were shocked to see that we were covered with big leeches.

I could make some puns about leeches, but they would probably suck.

Little Pleasant Lake

Once we tried out a new fishing lure at Big Pleasant Lake. It was called a Skitter Bait, and it was guaranteed to catch more fish than any other bait. Skitter Baits were quite noisy and were supposed to be reeled in very fast. I don't think we ever caught anything with the Skitter Baits, though.

We loved it when we got to go fishing with Daddy on those vacations, especially when he took us at night. He taught us to use only black lures when night fishing.

Pier on Little Pleasant Lake. (L-R) Tony, me, Mary Pat, Tom, and Margie

We also liked eating in the dining room at Pleasant Lake Lodge. The food was served family-style and was truly sumptuous. It was also the first time we ever got to drink iced tea.

The Wildwood Lodge also had delicious food. I bought a little souvenir wooden box from Wildwood Resort one year and kept treasures in that box at home in my dresser drawer for many years afterward.

Cabin at Wildwood Resort

Wildwood Resort. (L-R) Mary Pat, Sally Jo, me, Susan Jane, Tony, and Tommy.

Wildwood Resort was at the edge of a deep forest. We were all sure that there must have been big black bears all around us in that forest.

But there must not have been any bears there anymore, because when we were driving down the road to get there, we saw a fork in the road and a sign that said "Bear Left."

Once I saw a cross-eyed bear. Please bear with me, I just can't stop telling bear puns—I guess that is just a cross eye bear.

Sleeping Bear Sand Dunes. (L-R) Susie, me, Tom, Mike Valentine, and Tony

When we stayed at the Wildwood Resort, we would sometimes drive over to climb the really high Sleeping Bear Sand Dunes, which were not far away.

Traverse City Zoo. (L-R) Mommy, Sally Jo, and Susan Jane.

A Time of Innocence

We would also drive to nearby Traverse City to see a movie or go shopping. One year we went to the Traverse City Zoo.

Once when we were staying at the Wildwood Resort with the Valentine family, we took a boat ride on Lake Michigan.

Lake Michigan boat ride. (L-R) Tom, Susie, me, Sally Jo, Tony, Rusty Valentine, Jane Valentine, Mike Valentine, Pat Valentine, and Mary Pat

On left: Susan Jane on horse and Sally Jo standing next to her

One time at Wildwood Resort, a photographer took pictures of Sally Jo and Susan Jane on horses. They put those pictures on Wildwood Resort postcards

One of my favorite treats of all time was maple sugar candy, which we would buy while on vacation in Michigan. Once while riding in the back seat of our Chevy station wagon, I got in a little trouble for eating a whole box of maple sugar candy all by myself.

Wisconsin Dells postcards and brochures

A Time of Innocence

One year we had a great time vacationing at the Wisconsin Dells, which was on the way to Necedah, Wisconsin. We stayed at a motel there and rode the sightseeing boats on the Wisconsin River in order to see the Lower Dells. There we saw incredible sandstone formations, including the Arrow Head, the Devil's Football, the Milk Bottle, and the Sugar Bowl. The captain let Tommy drive the boat for a short time. We also visited Fort Dells, the Indian Trading Post, and the nearby amazing Wonder Spot, where it seemed as though you couldn't stand up straight.

We had to take the toll road to get to the Wisconsin Dells. Yes, you guessed it…we knew for whom the Dells tolled.

Chapter 26: Dining Room and New Room

Our family always ate meals together in the dining room. We said the blessing before every meal, and sometimes I would cry if I couldn't be the one to say it. If Tommy and I said the blessing together, afterward we would both say, "I said it best!" We also said a prayer after meals.

Family at old, round dining room table. (L-R) Tony, Sally Jo, Mommy, me, Tom, and Susie

Family sitting at new pine dining room tables (L-R): Mary Pat, Tom, Tony, Dad, Mom, me, Susie, and Margie.

A Time of Innocence

Tony didn't like peas, or many other vegetables for that matter. If he didn't like something on his plate—and if he thought no one was looking—he would toss the food over his shoulder onto the shelves behind him.

Although Tony liked to throw peas over his shoulder, he left most of them on his plate because he did not want to get in trouble for disturbing the peas. Sometimes though, he would just stuff the peas into his ears to plug them, because he wanted some peas and quiet.

We also played cards and board games around the dining room table.

I liked to play tricks on my brothers and sisters, putting dribble glasses, collapsing knives and forks, and fake ice cubes with flies in them on the dining room table before everyone sat down to eat.

Dribble glass

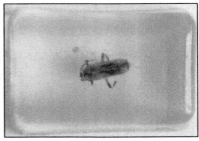
Fly in fake ice cube

We liked to race little plastic horses on the dining room table, on a race track we made on a big hardboard. We named our little horses after our favorite race horses: Whirlaway, Seabiscuit, Citation, and Man o' War.

Plastic race horses

Whirlaway

A Time of Innocence

Man o' War

There was a bread box on one of the shelves in the dining room, where our parents kept candy bars under lock and key. Tom, who was very clever, secretly made a master key that could open the lock, so that he could get into the bread box and get candy any time he wanted.

Tom found that knowing how to break into locks like that opened many doors for him later on in life. It was not surprising that he could do that, because in basketball, he could always set good picks at the top of the key.

Mommy and Daddy would often sit in the dining room and drink whiskey sours after we all went to bed. They probably needed to unwind after another day of raising seven of us.

Mommies like to unwind sometimes. It has been said that mummies like to unwind, too.

One year our parents had a closed-in porch built on the back side of our house. It had another bathroom and a closet. Thereafter, it was always called the "new room." It had knotty pine wood on the walls, just like our dining room, and that reminded me of the lodges where we stayed in Michigan. There were cabinets all along one wall, and they made great hiding places when we played hide-and-seek.

There was a trap door on the floor that went down to the crawl space under the new room, and that also made a really good hideout. We thought we might need to hide there, too, if we ever got attacked by the Russians.

We might have been Russian to conclusions, but we believed we didn't have much time to prepare for an attack, so there could be no Stalin around. We knew the Russians might attack us, because we got high Marx in school and Red about it in the paper. But if the Russians were going to attack us, then Soviet!

When I was about seven, and after we had built the new room, I said, "Someday our woods are going to be all full of our house."

A Time of Innocence

Chapter 27: The Eye Doctor

This chapter is dedicated to my dear friend Dr. Tom Funk. Tom is an incredible optometrist—and also an avowed punster.

When my parents took me to the eye doctor, I tried to memorize the eye chart when I walked past it. But that didn't fool my eye doctor at all.

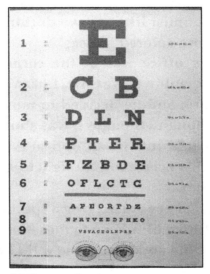

1940s eye chart

I cried the first day I had to wear glasses, because I really didn't want to wear them. But at the same time I was amazed that, for the first time ever, I could actually see the leaves on the trees.

Eye went to our family doctor and told him that eye was seeing spots in front of my eyes. He asked me if I had seen an eye doctor yet. I said, "No, I haven't seen an eye doctor, I've only seen spots."

The first time I met my optometrist, I asked, "Eye doctor?", and he answered, "What a coincidence—I doctor, too!" The receptionist had asked me to sign in, and to be sure to dot my T's and cross my eyes, so I did, and that was why my eye doctor and eye did not always see eye-to-eye.

But I liked his assistant, whose name was Iris. When I squinted my eyes and looked at her, Iris looked a lot like that famous movie actress, Angela Lensblurry. Iris tried to teach me all about the eye. She said I was her prize pupil.

If I was having trouble with my vision, when I got to the eye doctor's office I would always say, "Long time, no see." I wanted to be an optimist like my eye doctor, so I asked him to give me a pair of rose-colored glasses.

My eye doctor's office was at the cornea of Buffalo and Center Street in downtown Warsaw. But my eye doctor was a peripheral visionary, and he decided to move to some islands next to Alaska, although I thought it was short-sighted, because then the doctor would just be an optical Aleutian. In Alaska, though, the people do need good ice sight to spot glaciers, which is really a Titanic job.

You may think that eye am making a spectacle of myself, and you may want to turn a blind eye to these puns. You may even want to lash out at me and hope I put a lid on the puns, but if you call the pun police, eye will just say, "Eye was framed!"

Chapter 28: Fishing, Swimming, and Lake Cottages

Daddy was an ardent fisherman. He often went fishing on Monday, his day off from work. He liked to go with one of his friends, Pinky McClellan, a mailman who had a small private lake not far from Warsaw. Sometimes Daddy took us to Pinky's lake to go fishing with him.

Daddy usually caught several largemouth bass at Pinky's lake. He had to keep a record for Pinky of every fish he caught.

Daddy told us about another lake where he also liked to go fishing. I don't remember the name of that lake, but Daddy said it was so deep that they couldn't even find the bottom.

Daddy taught us all about fishing. We loved this time we spent with him. We were so excited when he bought us our first spin casting fishing reels and rods that we practiced casting them for hours in our yard.

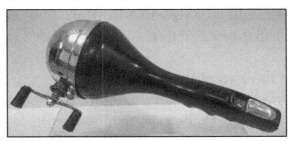

My first fishing reel

Daddy usually took us fishing on lakes around Warsaw, including Center Lake, Pike Lake, Winona Lake, and Chapman Lake. We had an Evinrude three-horsepower outboard motor. We mostly cast or trolled for bass or pike.

My favorite fishing lures were plastic worms and Johnson spoons.[32]

Some other favorite fishing lures

We often used bamboo poles, worms, and bobbers to still-fish for panfish such as blue gills, sunfish, perch, crappies, and rock bass.

One year we ordered a new bait to which you were supposed to add a scent that came with it. We didn't catch anything with that.

We should have scent the bait back.

One important thing Daddy taught us about fishing was, "When the wind is from the east, fishing is at its least; when the wind is from the west, fishing is at its best; when the wind is from the south, the bait floats in their mouth; and when the wind is from the north, no fish sally forth."

I thought we shouldn't take my sister Sally fishing with us when the wind was blowing from the north, because then no fish would Sally forth.

I just can't bass up the chance to tackle writing some reely good fish puns for all you buoys and gills. You may not want me to, but the die has been cast. Though I am not just fishing

for a compliment, I have had time to mullet over, and have salmoned up the strength to write several puns in a roe, because you really don't have to be a brain sturgeon to write puns. I fear, though, I may flounder, and don't know if my brain will snapper what. I don't want to carp about it, but I don't know if I am in the best pun grouper not, or if I am known trout the land as a great punster. There might be a debait about that. What if my puns are crappie and sole bad they smelt, and there were no better fish puns coming down the pike?

This is a different school of thought, but most people don't know that fish like music, and I have been herring rumors that some fish prefer Vince Gill's hits. Fish can practice scales and have been heard to play *Salmon Enchanted Evening, I'm a Sole Man*, and *Nearer My Cod to Thee*.

I must admit that sole is my favorite fish, because confession is good for the sole. I ordered fresh halibut once, but it came COD. You might say, "Oh, my Cod! He is making me eel and is gilling me with these puns!"

If you sea that I have hooked you on these fish puns, let minnow, but you have probably haddock with these puns. If you think I am gillty of writing too many fish puns, then I should be loxed up to balance the scales of justice. I can sardinely change my tuna, and try to scale back next time. But that's a different kettle of fish, and I am fin-ished now, because if I write any more puns, you might batter me, and I have other fish to fry.

Our family would sometimes go swimming at Island Park on Big Chapman Lake. Big Chapman Lake and Little Chapman Lake were only a few miles from Warsaw. We often took our goggles, fins, and snorkels with us to go snorkeling. Tom liked to also go spear-fishing at Island Park.

One year, when we rented a cottage at Island Park on Big Chapman Lake, Daddy caught a monster northern pike while trolling with a green flatfish lure. They put a picture of Daddy holding the pike in the *Warsaw Times-Union* newspaper.

Daddy holding large pike.

When we were younger, Mommy took us swimming at Pike Lake, since it was the closest lake with a beach. Sometimes we would go to Center Lake because they had a better beach, as well as big swings, teeter-totters, and a merry-go-round.

A Time of Innocence

When we went to the beach, we all got along swimmingly.

Front yard. (L-R) Sally Jo, Susan Jane, Tommy, me, and Tony

Center Lake Beach. (L-R) Me, Susan Jane, Tommy, and Sally Jo.

We didn't often go swimming at Winona Lake, but when we did, they had a rule that boys had to wear white tee-shirts. The town of Winona Lake was well-known as a religious community, influenced by the famous evangelist and baseball player Billy Sunday.

Entrance to park at Winona Lake

We had our high school graduation ceremony in the Billy Sunday Tabernacle at Winona Lake.

Billy Sunday Tabernacle

Once we built a little swimming pool by the side of our house. We dug a big hole and mixed some cement for the inside of the pool. The cement, though, was really rough on our feet, so we didn't swim in the pool much. There was no way to drain the pool, so after a while the water got really stagnant.

We were all thrilled when our parents bought two furnished cottages next to each other on Little Chapman Lake.

Our two cottages on Little Chapman Lake

Margie and Mary Pat playing baseball at cottage on Little Chapman Lake.

Our grandparents, Mamaw and Pappy, moved into one of the cottages, and we began staying in the other cottage during the summertime.

We had to clear out the brush down by the lake. Several of us got poison ivy rashes doing it. Tom and his friend, Dean Shively, built a raft for us, and we spent most of our days there swimming off the pier and raft. Sometimes we got leeches all over us.

Pier in front of our cottages. (L-R) Tony, Pappy, Margie, me, Tom, and Susie

I loved to go fishing on Little Chapman and Big Chapman Lakes, which were connected by a narrow channel. I liked to troll or cast my lures around the lily pads.

Tom made his own spear-fishing gun. He and Dean Shively would go spear-fishing together, looking for carp or garfish on Little Chapman Lake.

Once a garfish had really bad breath. Tom had never seen a garlic that!

A Time of Innocence

We had a lot of herons on our pier, and I really tended to harbor them. In fact, I seemed to have a heron addiction. To be Frank, "Egrets, I've had a few...but then again, too few to mention."

Chapter 29: Books, Magazines, and Newspapers

I always loved reading books. Groucho Marx once said, "Outside of a dog, a book is man's best friend; inside a dog, it's too dark to read."

Tommy, Tony, and I especially loved the Hardy Boys books. The first one I ever read was *The Mystery of Cabin Island*. My sisters mostly read Nancy Drew books.

I also read most of the Bobbsey Twins books. In addition, I liked the Chip Hilton sports books, Ken Holt mystery books, Tom Corbett Space Cadet books, and any of the Big Little Books.

Hardy Boys, Chip Hilton, Ken Holt, and Bobbsey Twins books

A Time of Innocence

Big Little Books

One of my favorite books of all time was *The Bears of Blue River*. Daddy used to read it to us at night. We especially liked the chapter about the little boy shooting the one-eared bear.

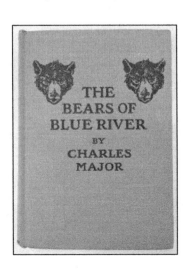

When I was older, one of my favorite books was *Magnificent Obsession*. It was written by Lloyd C. Douglas, who was born in Columbia City not far from Warsaw. It was a novel about a doctor who secretly performed good deeds, which gave him the spiritual power to become an outstanding physician. Later it was made into a movie starring Rock Hudson and Jane Wyman.

Some magazines I liked to read were *Readers Digest, Popular Mechanics, National Geographic,* and *Popular Science*.[33] We had a subscription to *Sports Illustrated* magazine and received the first issue (published in 1954).

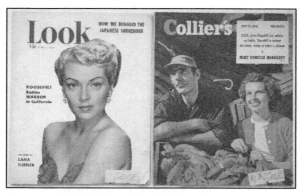

Look and Collier's magazines

A Time of Innocence

We also had subscriptions to *Life, Look, Colliers,* and *Saturday Evening Post* magazines, which I often read.

Favorite sports magazines

I also loved *Sport* magazines, as well as *The Sporting News* that I bought at Mumaw's newsstand downtown. Other sports magazines I liked to buy at Mumaw's were *Complete Baseball, Inside Sports, Sports Album, Sport Life,* and *Sports World.*

William R. Van Osdol, MD

The *Sporting News* newspaper

We also got a number of newspapers. In addition to the *Warsaw Times-Union* and the *Fort Wayne Journal Gazette*, we also received the Catholic newspaper *Our Sunday Visitor*.

Our parents bought a set of Collier's encyclopedias that we kept in our living room in the bookcase under the front window. We used them often to look things up for school.

On Sunday mornings, after going to church, we would buy three different Sunday papers from the newsstand—the *Fort Wayne Journal Gazette*, *South Bend Tribune,* and *Chicago Tribune.*

When we brought the papers home, we would all shout out the name of the one we wanted to read first. I usually yelled, "Chicago Tribune!" because I liked to read the *Dick Tracy* and *Joe Palooka* comic strips, as well as the articles about the Chicago Cubs. I especially liked some of the characters in *Dick Tracy*, including Tess Trueheart, B.O. Plenty, Sparkle Plenty, Pruneface, and Breathless Mahoney. I also liked to save the *Dick Tracy Crime Stoppers* feature in the *Chicago Tribune*.

Other comic strips I liked to read were *Blondie, Little Orphan Annie, Li'l Abner,* and *Prince Valiant*.[34]

We always kept a stack of comic books in the closet in our bedroom. Some of my favorites were *Space Cadet, Alley Oop, Bugs Bunny,* and *Shmoo*.[35]

A Time of Innocence

Some favorite comic books

Chapter 30: Radio and TV

We listened to the radio a lot because we didn't have a television set in our home. Daddy always told us that we would get one when color TVs came out.

1950s Philco radio

It is a good thing that Philo Farnsworth invented the TV, because otherwise we would all still be eating radio dinners on radio trays.

Although we didn't have a TV, I knew that most of my friends liked to watch *The Ed Sullivan Show, I Love Lucy,* and *American Bandstand.*

I loved to listen to the Cubs games in the new room on WGN, the Chicago radio station. I really liked the game announcers Jack Quinlan and Lou Boudreau. Boudreau had played shortstop for the Cleveland Indians, had been a manager for several baseball teams, and was in the Baseball Hall of Fame.

A Time of Innocence

Lou Boudreau

I also liked to listen to the *The Lone Ranger, Mr. and Mrs. North, Dragnet, Sergeant Preston of the Yukon,* and *Gang Busters*.[36]

Sergeant Preston of the Yukon comic book   *Gang Busters* comic book

When I returned from catechism class on Saturday mornings, I usually listened to the *Gene Autry Show* and *B-Bar-B Ranch* on the radio.

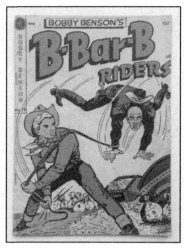

B-Bar-B Ranch comic book

I also listened to police reports over the shortwave radio on the desk in our bedroom. Our parents bought us that desk at an auction, and Tom built the console.

Rocky Marciano

A Time of Innocence

While in bed, I would listen to the heavyweight boxing fights on the radio. Rocky Marciano, Jack Dempsey, Joe Louis, Gene Tunney, Ezzard Charles, and Jersey Joe Walcott were some of my favorite boxers of all time.[37]

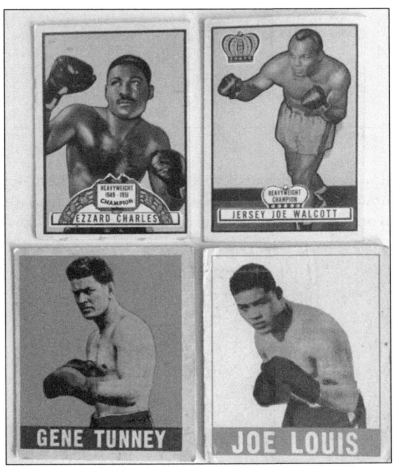

Boxing trading cards

I always listened to the Indianapolis 500 auto race on the radio. I kept a record of the leaders and those who were out of the race. My favorite driver was Bill Vukovich; I also liked A.J. Foyt, Sam Hanks, Rodger Ward, and Johnny Parsons.[38]

William R. Van Osdol, MD

Bill Vukovich

Following the Indianapolis 500 races, we would have our own race around the house on our bikes. We liked to pretend we were our favorite race car drivers. I always liked to be Bill Vukovich.

Chapter 31: The Milkman

The Crystal Dairy milkman, in his white cap and uniform, delivered oleo and milk in glass bottles to our side door. We were excited when he started bringing us homogenized milk, because it meant that we didn't have to shake it up anymore.

Crystal Dairy truck and milkman. (Photo courtesy of Michelle J. Bormet, *A History of the City of Warsaw, Indiana*)

If we could get rid of oleo, it has a curd to me that the world would be a whey butter place by a large margarine. You're probably thinking, "How dairy say that!" but I'm just trying to milk this for all its worth.

Mom checked every bottle of milk closely, and it would not get pasteurize if there was any spoiled milk or butter. She never churned them over to the Butter Business Bureau, either, because one good churn deserves an udder.

Once we had a minister in town who delivered pastorized milk.

We even had a farmer in town who could get chocolate milk out of his brown cows. That made us ask, "How now brown cow?" The farmer's name was Nestle and he was Quik when it came to milking those brown cows, although he did say the whole experience was draining.

Another dairy in Warsaw was Rife's, owned by our bus driver, Chauncey Rife. When Rife's Dairy started, the milk was delivered by a horse and wagon. One time the horse was frightened by a storm and ran through Oakwood Cemetery pulling a driverless wagon while scattering milk bottles everywhere.[39]

But there was no use crying over spilled milk.

Once when I was reading *A Tale of Two Cities* **and drinking a Carton of milk, I began to fear that if I wrote any more dairy puns, I too could be pun-ished and sent to the guillotine. That would be OK, though, because then I could udder, "It is a far, far butter thing that I do, than I have ever done."**

I'm sorry, I shouldn't have written that last pun. I just lost my head.

A Time of Innocence

Chapter 32: Movies

We owned a small movie projector and movie screen. We loved to watch 16 mm movies such as *Mickey Mouse*, *Felix the Cat*, and *Abbott and Costello* in the living room or new room.

We liked to go to the movies at the Strand Theatre on Saturday mornings. We got to see cowboy serials or the Bowery Boys shows there, sometimes for just ten cents. We also liked to go to the Lake and Centennial theaters. The Centennial Theatre later became the Boice Theatre. The most fun was when we all piled into our station wagon and went to the Warsaw Drive-In Theatre.

Centennial Theatre. (Photo courtesy of Michelle J. Bormet, *A History of the City of Warsaw, Indiana*)

1950s movie popcorn

One of my fondest memories of the movies was when we all went to the Lake Theatre with our parents to see the movie *Niagara*, starring Marilyn Monroe and Joseph Cotten.

Some of my favorite movie actors were Humphrey Bogart, Gary Cooper, and Kirk Douglas. My favorite movie actresses included Marilyn Monroe, Elizabeth Taylor, and Grace Kelly.[40]

Movie magazines. (L-R) Elizabeth Taylor and Marilyn Monroe

A Time of Innocence

Casablanca lobby card

Humphrey Bogart once walked by a Greek statue and said, "Here's looking at Euclid!" He was such a monumental actor. You probably think there should be a statue of limitations about such puns. This might be all Greek to you, too, because my Greek puns are so myth understood. But I am not going to Apollo-gize.

Some of my favorite movies included *The House of Wax* (the first 3D film in color), *The Ten Commandments, High Noon, Casablanca, From Here to Eternity, Bridge Over the River Kwai,* and *The Creature from the Black Lagoon.*[39]

From Here to Eternity lobby card

The Creature from the Black Lagoon lobby card

Once when I was eating a can of black beans, a small creature crawled out of the can. It was The Creature from the Black Legume.

I loved all the cowboy movies, especially those with John Wayne, Gene Autry, Roy Rogers, The Lone Ranger, or Hopalong Cassidy.

I saw about every Bowery Boys movie ever made, and most of the Three Stooges and Abbott and Costello movies, as well.

Bowery Boys lobby card

A Time of Innocence

My favorite cartoons (shown just before the movies) were *Mighty Mouse, Bugs Bunny, Tom and Jerry,* and *Woody Woodpecker.*

Chapter 33: Songs, Singers, Records, and Music

One of my favorite songs was "Oh, My Papa" by Eddie Fisher.

That song always makes me think about Daddy and brings tears to my eyes.

Some of my other favorite songs were "Tennessee Waltz," "Lady of Spain," "Theme from Moulin Rouge," "A Kiss to Build a Dream On," "High Noon," "Side by Side," and "Wheel of Fortune."[42]

When I was older, another favorite song was "The Green Green Grass of Home," by Tom Jones.

In fact I liked that song so much that I just couldn't get it out of my head. I finally went to see my doctor and said to him, "I have this problem. I can't stop singing the song 'The Green Green Grass of Home'."

My doctor said, "It sounds like you have a severe case of the Tom Jones Syndrome."

"Is it rare?" I asked.

"It's Not Unusual," he said.

Another song I loved to listen to (and occasionally sing) was "That's Amore," by Dean Martin. I liked to sing some of the lyrics, "When the moon hits your eye like a big pizza pie, that's amore."

Another version of that song goes, "When you swim in the sea and an eel bites your knee, that's a moray."

Some older songs I liked were "Star Dust," "I'll Be Seeing You," "Harbor Lights," "Some Enchanted Evening," and "Don't Fence Me In."[43]

When we were playing soldiers, we liked to sing "From the Halls of Montezuma" and "The Caissons Go Rolling Along."

A Time of Innocence

Some of my favorite silly songs were "The Thing" (Daddy especially liked that one), "Flying Purple People Eater," and "Stranded in the Jungle."[44]

When we were younger, we had a lot of favorite songs that we sang including "Down in the Meadow" (a rope skipping song), "Jimmy Crack Corn," "Row, Row, Row Your Boat," and "Found a Peanut."[45]

We had a player piano in the new room, and I liked to play the old piano rolls. Some of my favorite songs on the piano rolls were "General Pershing March," "Stardust," "Moonlight Serenade," and "Begin the Beguine."

Like most kids at that time, my favorite singer was Elvis Presley; my favorite Elvis songs were "Love Me Tender," "It's Now or Never," and "All Shook Up."

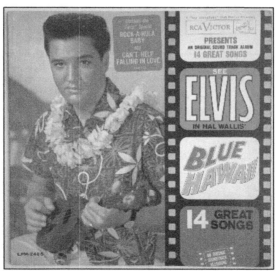

Elvis Presley record album

Other singers I especially liked were Ricky Nelson, Buddy Holly, Dean Martin, Patti Page, Rosemary Clooney, Johnny Mathis, Louis Armstrong, and Chuck Berry.[46]

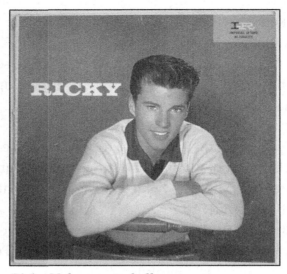

Ricky Nelson record album

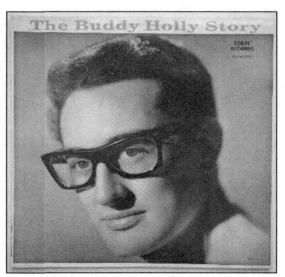

Buddy Holly record album

A Time of Innocence

Percy Faith record album

The Crew Cuts record album

    I also liked to listen to big bands such as Guy Lombardo, Glenn Miller, and Tommy Dorsey. My favorite LP album was *Bouquet*, by The Percy Faith Strings.

The Crew Cuts performed at our junior prom. Their most popular songs were "Earth Angel" and "Sh-Boom."

My favorite vocal groups were The Ink Spots, The Crew Cuts, Dion and the Belmonts, and The Four Freshmen.[47]

One of the Four Freshmen was from Warsaw. The group's most popular song was "It's a Blue World." The Four Freshmen liked to return to Warsaw, and they once performed at the Elks Club.[48]

Chapter 34: Nursery Rhymes and Fairy Tales

We loved to listen to Mommy or Daddy read us nursery rhymes and fairy tales. One of my favorites was "There Was an Old Woman Who Lived in A Shoe."[49]

You should know that these shoe puns are written with tongue in cheek. The old woman who lived in a shoe had so many children that they clogged up her house. The old woman, bless her sole, was not well-heeled, so she had to live on a shoestring budget. Her children liked to play with toads, because it was an open-toad shoe, but it made the old woman hopping mad because she was so straight-laced. She fed her children shoe-shi, cobbler, and shoestring potatoes without any bread, and sent them to bed. She worried the landlord might boot them out any time. Her health was not very good—she had clogs in her arteries. So even though their house was as comfortable as an old shoe, she decided to shoe all her children out of the house. They climbed into their Vans and moved into a small flat. The children said it was a Croc that they had to move. They all stuck their tongues out and said,"Ugg!" (Did eyelet you down with these shoe puns?)

Another one of my favorite nursery rhymes was "Humpty Dumpty."

Once Humpty Dumpty worked as a game warden and watched out for poachers. It was a terrible summer for him, but he had a great fall. It looked like Humpty had been beaten. Humpty said he sat on the wall because his friends egged him on to sit up there. The detectives scrambled to crack the case. They worried that they might have egg on their faces if they could not solve the crime. They knew there was a rhyme but no reason for the fall, and that the criminal they were after was probably planning his next rhyme, but they didn't want to go on a wild Mother Goose chase.

After his fall, Humpty went to see Dr. Benedict, who had a 2-minute egg appointment for him. Dr. Benedict whisked Humpty into an exam room and said, "You are a hard egg to crack. I can put you back together again, but I'm afraid I can't do anything about your cholesterol!"

Dr. Benedict liked his eggs served on hubcaps, because, "There's no plates like chrome for the Hollandaise."

I have a dear friend and colleague, Dr. Bryan Benedict, and he is indeed a good egg.

Another favorite nursery rhyme was "Pop Goes the Weasel."

I suppose you would like a pun about a weasel, too. OK… A weasel walks into a bar. The bartender asks, "What'll you have to drink?" "Pop," goes the weasel.

I also liked "Jack and Jill."

When Jack fell down and broke his crown, he had to go to the dentist and have a root canal. Most people don't know this, but Jack and Jill were the very first to have a Jack and Jill bathroom.

My favorite fairy tales were *Snow White and the Seven Dwarfs*, *Pinocchio*, and *Jack and the Beanstalk*.[50]

It is a little-gnome fact that 6 out of 7 dwarfs are not Happy.

When Pinocchio got his first haircut, he said to Geppetto, "I wood like a plane haircut."

We had a friend named Jack who helped us plant beans in our garden one year. We had to be wary about what we said, though, because you know, Jack and the beans talk.

A Time of Innocence

Chapter 35: Charles Atlas, Jiu Jitsu, Popeye, and Bosco

Tommy and I didn't want to be like that skinny weakling in the magazine ad who had sand kicked in his face by a bully on the beach. So we enrolled in the Charles Atlas Body-Building Course through the mail, in order to build up our muscles. (Heavyweight boxing champions Joe Louis and Rocky Marciano also took the Charles Atlas course.)[51]

Charles Atlas Body-Building Course

183

Dr. Frankenstein also once joined a body-building course, but he completely misunderstood the objective.

Charles Atlas was fond of saying, "Live clean, think clean, and don't go to burlesque shows."[52] We tried to follow those rules, at least for a while.

He also said, "I can make you a new man, too, in only 15 minutes a day!"[53] We believed that.

We did the work-out routine almost every day. It included a lot of knee bends, sit-ups, and push-ups. We <u>did</u> get stronger—no one ever kicked sand in our faces after that!

We also thought we needed to master the art of self-defense, so Tom and I sent for a jiu-jitsu course through the mail. We practiced it on each other every day for a while.

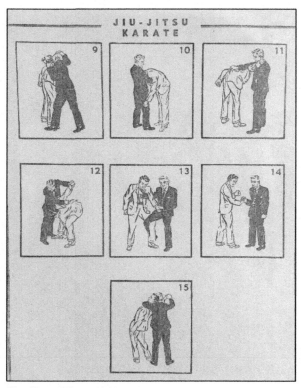

Jiu-jitsu illustrations

A Time of Innocence

Tom also had his own muscle building course. We had a contract, signed by both Tom and me, that said, "I am a member of Tom's Muscle Building Course."

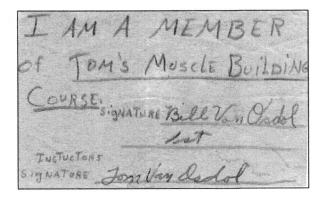

Another way we built up our muscles was by climbing up a long rope that we attached to a tree branch in the back yard by the shed.

We would sometimes rope Tony into doing it, once we had taught him the ropes.

We also liked to eat a lot of spinach so we could have muscles like Popeye.

Popeye comic book

When our parents noticed that all the cans of spinach were missing from the kitchen cabinets, we had to face the Spinach Inquisition.

We liked to put Bosco chocolate-flavored syrup in our milk every morning. It was supposed to give you "healthier bones, stronger muscles, and better teeth."[54] We actually believed all that.

This was the Bosco jingle:
"I love Bosco, it's rich and chocolaty,
Chocolate-flavored Bosco is mighty good for me!
Mama puts it in my milk for extra energy,
Bosco gives me iron and sunshine vitamin D!
Oh, I love Bosco, that's the drink for me!"[55]

Bosco was so popular that it was once mentioned in an episode of the TV series "M.A.S.H." Radar said his Aunt Mildred wouldn't let him dip his zwieback in his Bosco.[56]

I know this because *M.A.S.H.* used to be one of my favorite shows. I watched it Alda time.

People used to stop me in the street and ask, "Did anyone ever tell you that you look like Alan Alda?"

People still stop me in the street. But since I've lost a lot of hair, <u>now</u> they ask, "Did anyone ever tell you that you look like James Taylor?"

Chapter 36: Ovaltine and Captain Midnight

We liked to add Ovaltine to our milk. We thought that, like Bosco, drinking Ovaltine would help build up our muscles. Ovaltine was the sponsor for the Little Orphan Annie and Captain Midnight radio series, as well as the Howdy Doody Show on TV.

Howdy Doody Ovaltine cup

Some famous athletes, including Duke Snider (star outfielder for the Brooklyn Dodgers), "Crazylegs" Hirsch (great running back for the Los Angeles Rams), and Florence Chadwick (who swam the English Channel) were all in the "Captain Midnight Secret Squadron Hall of Fame." Of course, they all said you should drink your Ovaltine every day. You had to mix it exactly right in order to "give you rocket power."[57]

I, too, was a member of the Captain Midnight Secret Squadron and wore an official Secret Squadron patch. I also had a Captain Midnight secret ring decoder that I got by sending in labels from Ovaltine.

Captain Midnight's Secret Squadron manual

When I recently asked my brother Tom to describe me when I was growing up, he said, "There was always something about the little boy Ralphie, in the movie 'A Christmas Story,' that reminded me of you."

It is true that I liked to drink Ovaltine just like Ralphie. In addition, Ralphie had a Little Orphan Annie secret decoder, and I had a Captain Midnight secret decoder.

Also just like Ralphie, I liked to say, "I double-dog dare you!" to Tommy and Tony. I had bad eyes, and I always had to wear glasses like Ralphie did, as well.

And also like Ralphie, I sometimes got into trouble as I was growing up. As mentioned earlier, I chopped the legs off the antique table in our basement and got in some fights. Once I threw a rock and cracked the front windshield on our station wagon as Daddy was pulling our car into the driveway.

I also wanted an official Red Ryder carbine action, 200-shot, range model BB-gun for Christmas. I remember Mom saying about the BB-gun, "You'll shoot your eye out!"—just like Ralphie's mom.

I have a beautiful leg lamp downstairs now, just like the one Ralphie's father won and put in his front window. Mine has not been accidently broken yet.

So, yes, I must agree with my brother, Tom. I really was a lot like little Ralphie.

By the way, Tom also said he remembered me as funny, clever, and athletic—and that I loved and respected my family. (I'm especially proud of the last item on this list.)

William R. Van Osdol, MD

Chapter 37: Breakfast Cereals and Eggs

Our favorite breakfast cereals were Wheaties (because it was the "Breakfast of Champions"), Shredded Wheat, Grape Nuts, Puffed Rice, and Puffed Wheat.[58]

Shredded Wheat and Puffed Wheat

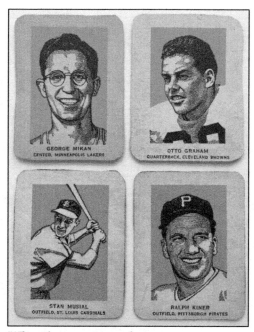

Wheaties sports cards

A Time of Innocence

I liked to cut the sports cards from the back of the Wheaties boxes. Some of my favorites were Ted Williams, Johnny Lujack, Doak Walker, Stan Musial, and Ben Hogan.[59]

We also collected the Injun-Uities cards from inside Shredded Wheat boxes.

We would get great prizes in cereal boxes—or we could send in the box tops for prizes. Some of our prizes were little comic books, frogmen and submarines that ran on baking soda, and tin license plates of all the states.[60]

Cereal box prizes

Among our most prized possessions were deeds for one square inch of land in the Yukon, from the Klondike Big Inch Land

Company. Tommy and I got them by sending in box tops from Quaker Puffed Wheat.

Deed of land from Klondike Big Inch Land Company

I thought that surely someday, after I grew up, I would go to the Yukon and find my land. Later, though, I found out that none of the Klondike deeds had actually been registered. So I never actually owned any land in the Yukon, after all. (Guess I'll forget that trip…)

But I still love to eat Klondike ice cream bars. And any puns about Canadian territories? It so happens I snow some, but Shirley Yukon be serious.

Tommy and I used to take turns cooking breakfast for each other before school. Tommy always wanted his eggs fried hard. I wanted my eggs sunny side up.

When Tommy asked me if I knew how to cook eggs, I said, "Omelet smarter than you think."

I know I shouldn't crack any more egg jokes, but it isn't really hard to do. If we got up too late, we had to scramble to finish eating our eggs, or we would miss the bus, and that would be no yoking matter.

I decided before my senior year in high school that I needed to be stronger and have more muscles to play on the basketball team. So I started making myself an egg nog drink out of 10 eggs every morning. I drank it all down at one time.

I wanted to be like Babe Ruth. He liked to eat 18-egg omelets for breakfast.

I didn't really get bigger muscles, but Dr. Baum said I had the highest cholesterol he ever saw!

Chapter 38: Doctors and Red Medicine

We all really loved our family doctor, Dr. Baum. He was a kind, compassionate, and dedicated physician. It was said that he was on call for his patients every day for about 20 years before he finally took a vacation.[61]

When I was older, my doctor told me I needed exercise. But I gained weight, because I thought he said I needed "extra fries." Then he said I needed more cardio, and I thought he meant playing my car radio more. My doctor also said I needed to run more, but I thought he said I needed to "pun more."

After all that, my doctor told me I needed a hearing test, but I thought he said I had a "hairy chest."

I decided to go on a banana diet to try to lose weight. All I ate were bananas—three for breakfast, three for lunch and three for dinner—it was an appeeling diet. In the end I didn't lose any weight, but you should have seen me climb trees!

Once I did decide to join an Iron Man Competition. I was proud because I was able to iron ten shirts in an hour.

There is some irony in that pun.

Sometimes I liked to see how far I could jump off the cement steps at the side of our house. Once when I jumped, I fell really hard and cut my lip and mouth. I had to go see Dr. Baum to be sutured up. Even though my lip hurt and was badly swollen, I was still proud because I had broken my record on how far I could jump off the porch.

I had another doctor once who liked to tell jokes. He was a real cut-up and he kept me in stitches. Once when I had a cut in my mouth, I tried to tell the doctor where the cut was, but I couldn't remember. Turns out it was right on the tip of my tongue. Then I tried to ask the doctor if he was going to use nylon or catgut to sew me up, but I couldn't get the words out and he asked, "Catgut your tongue?" It made me sew mad, I said I would suture my own cut, and the doctor said, "Suture self, I probably can't suture fancy anyway!"

We all dreaded having to have "red medicine" put on our scrapes and cuts by Mommy. The red medicines were iodine, Merthiolate, and mercurochrome. They all would really sting, especially Merthiolate. Later, Mommy started using Bactine, which didn't sting quite so much.

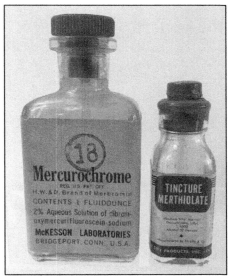

Red medicine—mercurochrome and Merthiolate

Once I swallowed a marble. Mommy had me eat lots of bread that day to try to get the marble to pass.

I don't think I ever passed that marble. That is probably why people tell me that I "don't have all my marbles."

I swallowed several coins once, too, but I didn't have any symptoms from the coins. The doctor said to call him if there was any change. He said it would just take dime for the coins to pass, but I should pass them within 24 hours. Otherwise I would be a day late and a dollar short. I thought that made a lot of cents. The doctor also told us that as long as I hadn't swallowed any counterfeit coins I should be OK, because counterfeit coins are harder to pass. The doctor refused to charge us much for his advice, saying that he wouldn't nickel and dime us.

He also told me that if I passed any pennies, I should save them in an urn because, to coin a phrase, "A penny saved is a penny urned."

Chapter 39: The County Fair

One of the highlights of our summers was going to the Kosciusko County Fair. During the rest of the year, we saved up our money in little banks to spend at the fair.

Some of our little banks

The fair was always a place of wonderment for us. We enjoyed going to the concession stands to get cotton candy, snow cones, salt water taffy, and caramel apples. Some of our favorite rides were the Tilt-a-Whirl, the Ferris Wheel, and the Rocket.[62] When we were younger, we liked riding the little cars, the airplanes, and the merry-go-round.

We loved playing the midway games, such as throwing ping pong balls into fishbowls (the fish didn't live very long when we took them home), playing the horse races (where we could win little cast copper horses), and shooting rifles.[63] Tom especially liked shooting rifles, and he was always a great shot.

Copper horse prize I won at the County Fair

We loved going through the haunted house and the house of mirrors. We also liked to go to the arcade to get Exhibit baseball cards out of the vending machines; these were about the size of postcards and were either black and white or sepia colored. Some of my favorite Exhibit baseball cards were Stan Musial, Ted Williams, Mickey Mantle, Satchel Paige, Jackie Robinson, Minnie Minoso, and Bob Lemon.[64]

Walking through the merchants building and the farm animal barns was also great fun. We were fascinated by the side shows, but we never went into them.

County Fair side shows

A Time of Innocence

We won some really nice chalk statue prizes at the fair, including statues of dogs, sailors, and horses.[65]

Some of our chalk statue prizes from the County Fair

It would be a fair statement to say, "You could chalk it up to good luck that we won so many statues."

Chapter 40: Holidays

Easter was always one of my favorite holidays. On the day before Easter, Holy Saturday, we would excitedly color eggs for the Easter bunny to hide. Our dining room smelled like vinegar for days.

We usually gave up eating candy for Lent, so we couldn't wait until noon on Holy Saturday because then we could start eating the candy we had saved up.

My favorite Easter songs were "Here Comes Peter Cottontail" and "The Easter Parade."

On Easter morning, we would hunt the Easter baskets and eggs that the Easter bunny had hidden in our living room. After finding all the eggs, we would then go to church; this was always special, because we all knew that we were celebrating the Resurrection of Jesus that day.

Easter decorations

A Time of Innocence

Some eggs that were very well-hidden weren't found until months later, when they were really rotten.

One year the Easter bunny left us some baby chicks; sadly one of them fell down the register. Also, I climbed into the box of chicks and accidently squashed one.

We looked forward to Halloween every year. We could hardly wait to go trick-or-treating and usually went by ourselves. (It was definitely a safer time.) We would sometimes start trick-or-treating as early as a full week before Halloween. We usually wore just scary rubber masks, which were sometimes hard to see through. When I was very young, I especially liked to wear a skeleton costume.

Halloween pumpkin

We would walk into the east side of town and trick-or-treat at the houses on Market, Center, Main, and Fort Wayne Streets, until we got tired or it got late. Most people were friendly to us when they answered their doors, and they often asked us our names. We knew where some of the grumpy people lived, and we would avoid going to their houses. One time we were chased by a man who tried to spray us with his water hose.

The treats we got were mostly candy bars such as Heath, Clark, Sky Bar, and Milky Way. We also got Cracker Jacks and lots of candy corn.

We didn't play any truly mean tricks for Halloween. We did soap (or throw corn at) neighborhood windows, but we never soaped screens (since it was almost impossible to remove the soap). We also had fun sticking car horns. My friend Bill "Hoovie" Hoover came up with the idea of sticking horns using athletic tape. (In remembering that time, Hoovie once said, "October, burning leaves, coolness in the air, and blaring horns—a teenage heaven!")

One year some of my friends got into a little trouble for crushing some watermelons. (Most people don't know this, but the record for the most watermelons crushed with your head in one minute is 43!)

Thanksgiving was also a memorable holiday for us. Our grandparents, Mamaw and Pappy, and Uncle Russy and Aunt Ede usually came over for dinner, and Mom always cooked a big turkey with all the trimmings.

Sometimes we traveled down to Elwood on Thanksgiving Day to visit the Kiefers, including Aunt Sarah (Mamaw's sister), Uncle John, and our cousins. One year Mom wrote a poem about visiting the Kiefers on Thanksgiving (see Appendix D).

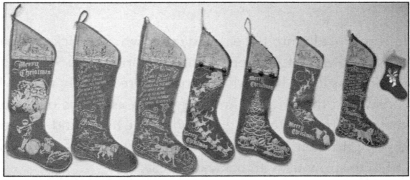

Our Christmas stockings

A Time of Innocence

Christmas was the most wondrous and joyous time of all for us. We hung our seven Christmas stockings on the fireplace with our letters to Santa Claus inside. We also had a special little stocking for our dog Nellie.

Daddy always went out and bought a live Christmas tree a few days before Christmas. We cut off the bottom and brought the tree into the house. We all helped to carefully hang our treasured ornaments, decorations, and lights on the tree. One year in school I made an angel that I enjoyed hanging on the tree.

My Christmas angel

Christmas 1943. (L-R) Daddy holding Tommy, Susan Jane and Sally with their dolls, and Pappy holding me. The sign on the floor, "C. Dean Van Osdol," was later hung in our front yard by the road.

Sign by the side of the road

A Time of Innocence

Christmas 1954. (L-R) Susie, Sally, Mary Pat, me, Tony, Tom, and Margie

It was a special time when we set up the little nativity scene by the fireplace. It was always a reminder that Christmas was the day we celebrated the birth of Jesus.

Nativity set

I loved all of the traditional Christmas songs. My favorite ones when I was younger were "I Want a Hippopotamus for Christmas," "Rudolph the Red Nosed Reindeer," and "Frosty the Snowman." When I was older, I liked "Santa Claus Is Coming to Town," "Here Comes Santa Claus," and "Jingle Bells."[66] One of my favorite Christmas carols was "Silver Bells." I also especially liked "Silent Night," "Joy to the World," "Away in a Manger," and "The First Noel."[67]

Our parents always hid our Christmas gifts in the attic when we were very young. We had to climb up a very steep ladder in the kitchen closet to get to the attic, so — especially when we were young — we didn't go up there very often. The attic was filled with all kinds of treasures including Uncle Russy's Navy uniform. One year Tommy discovered our Christmas presents when he happened to go up into the attic. Then we knew there really wasn't a Santa Claus. But we didn't tell our little sisters, Mary Pat and Margie, what Tommy had found.

It has been said that Santa had low elf esteem be claus his parents told him when he was born that he did not exist.

Mom and Daddy kept busy shopping for us. Mom lovingly sent out Christmas cards to all of our friends. It was such a joyful time wrapping gifts for each other a few days before Christmas.

One year I bought a *Big Little Book* for Tommy from Haffner's five-and-ten store. Before wrapping it, I found out that Tommy really wanted a collapsible plastic knife. So the next day I went back to Haffner's and exchanged the *Big Little Book* for a plastic knife.

On Christmas Eve, Mom would always help us put out cookies and milk next to the fireplace for Santa Claus. After going to bed, we listened for sleigh bells until we finally fell asleep.

When we woke up Christmas morning, we would all jump out of bed and, with much anticipation, hurry into the living room to see what Santa Claus had brought us. It was so exciting to find wonderful toys and other gifts from Santa under the tree and in our stockings.

Later, after going to church, we would open our wrapped gifts from one another and from Mom and Daddy. When Uncle Russy, Aunt Ede, Mamaw, and Pappy came over, we would exchange gifts with them, as well.

One year I went shopping before Christmas with Daddy at the Hull House clothing store in downtown Warsaw. I saw a dark maroon and white cardigan sweater in the store that I really liked, so I tried it on. I knew it cost too much, so I didn't ask for it for Christmas.

Then on Christmas, when I opened my gifts from Mom and Daddy, I was completely surprised to see that they had given me that very same maroon and white cardigan sweater. I realized that Daddy had gone back later to the store to buy it for me. That was always my favorite sweater and very special to me. I always thought lovingly about Daddy whenever I wore that cardigan.

Mom and me in my maroon and white sweater

One time when I was wearing that sweater while driving, a policeman pulled up beside me and said, "Pull over." I said, "No, it's a cardigan, but thanks for noticing." And once I tried to buy another sweater with my Visa card, but I had to swipe the cardigan.

We spent most of the rest of Christmas day playing with our new toys, trying on our new clothes, or reading our new books.

Tom with Christmas gifts in 1955, including a spin cast fishing reel, Mr. Wizard's Science Secrets, hockey sticks, ice skates, a pump pellet gun, and *Hardy Boys*, *Ken Holt*, and *Space Cadet* books.

Tom and Jerry drink set

A Time of Innocence

Then after a big dinner, Mom and Daddy usually made hot Tom and Jerry drinks. Of course, only the grown-ups got to add whiskey to theirs (see Appendix B).

Usually someone gave us a nice fruitcake at Christmas, but I didn't eat much of it.

Most people don't know it, but there was actually a fourth wise man, who was turned away for bringing a fruitcake. You are probably now thinking that I am nuttier than a fruitcake for making jokes that just take the cake.

Another highly anticipated holiday was the Fourth of July, when we enjoyed celebrating our country's independence. When evening came, we lit our sparklers, black snakes, and other fireworks in the front yard. When it got darker, we all climbed into our station wagon, and Daddy and Mom drove us to the fairgrounds to watch the fireworks. We especially enjoyed watching the grand finale.

Fourth of July sparklers

On Armistice Day (later called Veteran's Day), we liked to watch the military parade as it passed down Main Street. There were marching bands, festive floats, proud veterans, heavy tanks, parade horses, prominent city officials, cheering crowds, and children waving small flags. We all loved these parades.

1940s handheld 48-star parade flags

In grade school, Valentine's Day was always special for me. In class we would take turns decorating a large cardboard box with wrapping paper, ribbons, and cut out hearts. On Valentine's Day we would drop our valentines into the box. Someone from the class was then chosen to deliver the valentines to each of us.

The valentines were colorful and funny, and they often included poems, rhymes, cartoon characters, military themes, Indians, or moving parts. I treasured my valentines and usually kept them until the next year.

A Time of Innocence

1940s valentines

William R. Van Osdol, MD

Chapter 41: Downtown

When we were growing up, downtown Warsaw had many wonderful stores and restaurants.

At the Humpty Dumpty restaurant we could get great cheeseburgers, fries, and milkshakes. Fred Olds, a beloved local teacher, coach, and artist, painted beautiful wall murals in that restaurant.

1950s Humpty Dumpty restaurant menu

A Time of Innocence

Humpty Dumpty restaurant. (Photo courtesy of Michelle J. Bormet, *A History of the City of Warsaw, Indiana*)

Walter's Drug Store. (Photo courtesy of Indiana Album)

Walter's Drug Store also had great burgers, fries, malts, shakes, and cherry cokes. I liked listening to the song "The Yellow Rose of Texas" played on the store's juke box.

Penguin Point restaurant. (Photo courtesy of Michelle J. Bormet, *A History of the City of Warsaw, Indiana*)

We also loved to go to the Penguin Point drive-in. It was known for its giant breaded tenderloins and was where all the kids would gather when they were old enough to drive. Another popular spot was the B & K Root Beer stand, which served delicious root beer floats.

The Flagpole was a wonderful frozen custard stand. My favorite flavor was lemon. Their signature treat was called a Flagpole Special, which was made of vanilla custard covered with chocolate, nuts, and a cherry. They also had a large banana split that they called a "Pig's Dinner." If you could finish it while sitting there, you would get a pin that said "I Ate a Pig's Dinner at the Flagpole." After eating nine Pig's Dinners, you got the 10th one free. They also had a Suicide Sundae with eight scoops of frozen custard.[68,69]

A Time of Innocence

Flagpole Drive-In owner Joe Johnson pauses in front of his restaurant which became popular for its frozen custard. Signs in the window picture the "Pig's Dinner" and other delicious desserts.

These buttons could be turned in at the Flagpole for a free "Pig's Dinner" when hungry patrons had collected ten buttons.

The Flagpole Drive-In frozen custard stand. (Photo courtesy of Michelle J. Bormet, *A History of the City of Warsaw, Indiana*)

They also served a tin roof sundae at the Flagpole. You could say they really nailed it with that recipe, and it was the shingle-best sundae they made. Although the price was usually through the roof, sometimes we didn't have to pay anything because they said the tin roof sundae was on the house.

I loved to buy the *Sporting News* newspaper at Mumaws Newsstand. We all liked to shop at W. R. Thomas and Haffner's five-and-ten stores. We often bought one another Christmas gifts there.

It was always a thrill for us to go to Essig's sporting goods store, where we bought all of our baseballs, softballs, bats, mitts, footballs, basketballs, and other sports equipment. The owner, Sport Essig, was a classmate of Daddy's in high school.

1950s softball and baseball

There was also the Liberty Café (where they had dribble glasses and trick knives and forks on the tables), the Favorite Café, Judd's Drug Store, Unique Bakery, and Breading's Cigar Store (owned by Louis Breading, our Little League baseball coach).

Right under Breading's Cigar Store was Knoop's Barbershop, where I got my haircuts. Russell Knoop's son, Tom, played baseball and basketball with me in high school. Rusty Valentine, one of our parents' best friends, worked for a while at the same barbershop.

Mr. Knoop graduated at the head of his class in barber school. He was always Head and Shoulders above the rest of the barbers.

I would usually get a crew cut or a flat top haircut at the barbershop. Later I had a "ducktail" with my flat top; I had to use a lot of Butch Hair Wax to keep it all in place.

Butch Hair Wax

Hull House clothing store. (Photo courtesy of Indiana Album)

The town's first discount store was the Wonder Store, where we sometimes bought clothes for school. Other favorite clothing stores were Hull House, Phipps, and Stephenson's department stores.

We liked to watch the Soap Box Derby every year in downtown Warsaw, and one year Daddy was an inspector for the cars. The Benson brothers were famous for winning these races. Dale Benson won the race one year, and his brother Jay won the following year. Dale's other brothers, Paul and Dan, also won the Derby in later years.[70,71,72] The Soap Box Derby was a great experience for many boys across the country.

Soap Box Derby. (L-R) Dale Benson and Jay Benson

OK, I will get off my soap box now.
Dale Benson later became a dear life-long friend.

Chapter 42: Hobbies and Pastimes

One of my hobbies was collecting rock fossils. On lazy summer days, I often rode my bicycle over to a gravel pit a few miles away, where I would spend hours looking for fossils in the rocks for my collection. That was always a peaceful and enjoyable time for me.

Some people just don't like puns about rocks, and those used to be my sediments exactly. Over time, however, I decided I liked rock puns, and that put me between a rock and a hard place about writing them. I really wanted to write puns about rocks, but I didn't want to gravel about it. But I got a little boulder and went ahead and dug up some of these puns that will rock you.

I liked to go rock hunting for fossils when it was a gneiss day. I always took the rock hunting kit that I bought on shale, because I did not want to leave a stone unturned. I usually packed a lunch because I had a good apatite.

The time I needed to be home from rock hunting wasn't set in stone. I wore my Fossil watch so I wouldn't stay too long, because I didn't want anyone to quarry me about it. I will take it for granite that you would like me to end these puns, and say, as the Jedi might have said, "May the quartz be with you!"

Another of my favorite hobbies was juggling. I ordered a juggling kit through the mail, and I loved to practice juggling the little yellow rubber balls that came with the kit. I was finally able to juggle four of them at one time.

William R. Van Osdol, MD

1950s juggling kit. (Photo courtesy of David Cain)

When I was in junior high school, I was in a talent show to demonstrate how I could juggle. I started out juggling four balls for a few minutes. Then they turned the lights out. By using a black light and fluorescent yellow paint on round cardboard cut-outs I had made and attached to strings, I gave the illusion that I was juggling five balls in each hand at the same time.

In a more jocular vein, I was always afraid if people didn't like my juggling, they might go for my juggler!

Other performers in the talent show that night were Susie Mollenhour and Patty Mulcahy, two of my classmates, who put on a pantomime of Patience and Prudence singing their hit song, "Tonight You Belong to Me."

I had a lot of other hobbies and pastimes, as well.

In fact, it was a juggling act for me to keep track of them all.

Another favorite pastime was entering contests. I subscribed to a contest magazine and would eagerly enter almost every contest I could find, hoping against all odds that someday I would win a big prize. Although I sent in a lot of box tops and labels, I almost never won anything. The only contest in which I ever won a prize was for naming a pony. I named it "Himbuktu" and won a cap-shooting toy rifle with a telescopic sight. (Truth be known, it was actually Mom who suggested the name for me.)

(L-R) Margie, Tony holding Pudgy, and Mary Pat holding my cap-shooting toy rifle with telescopic sight

Once when I was listening to the local radio station (WRSW) with Mom and Daddy, the station had a contest in which they asked, "In what kind of robbery are you least likely to be caught?" Daddy told me I should go ahead and call in my answer, so I did. I told the announcer that my answer was, "Robbing the cradle." But I didn't win the prize; the correct answer was, "A safe robbery."

Some of my other hobbies and pastimes included: playing almost every sport; collecting Indian head nickels, baseball cards, and *Dick Tracy Crime Stoppers*; listening to the radio; reading; writing stories; writing to pen pals; and keeping a sports scrapbook.

William R. Van Osdol, MD

My brothers and I all started collecting baseball cards in 1952, and they became our prized possessions. There was nothing more exciting than opening up a new pack of Topp's baseball cards with bubble gum inside. Topps cards were always my favorite, although I also liked the Bowman's cards. From my cards, I learned the names of just about every major league baseball player. I also collected football cards. Sometimes I took some of my cards on the school bus to trade with other kids.

Unopened pack of 1951 baseball cards

I had a pen pal who lived in the Gold Coast in Africa. One time he sent me some real pieces of gold, which I greatly treasured.

S&H Green Stamps and Top Value Stamps, which could be redeemed for merchandise, were given out at almost all businesses. I liked sticking them in the stamp books, and we all took turns doing that.

A Time of Innocence

S&H Green Stamps

But if I didn't get to put the stamps in the books, I would get mad and stamp my feet!

I loved taking photos with the Kodak Brownie Hawkeye flash camera that I got for my birthday one year. I soon became the family photographer. I also took pictures with the midget camera that I ordered from the *Johnson Smith Catalog of Novelties.*

Kodak Brownie Hawkeye camera

I took some photos of the farmlands around us, but they were really grainy. I kept the photos anyway, because I didn't want to go against the grain.

Once we decided to take a picture of Tommy shooting my cowboy hat off my head with his cap gun. We threw a string over a tree branch above me and attached one end of the string to my hat; I held the other end of the string with one hand. Just as Tommy "shot" at me with his cap gun, I pulled on the string to raise the hat off my head while Susan Jane snapped our picture with my camera.

Tommy shooting cowboy hat off my head

Once when we were hiking in Alaska, I took a photo of a big brown bear. It was a Kodiak moment.

Chapter 43: Summer Jobs

My first summer job was working as a park policeman at Center Lake Park. I mostly roamed the park and hung out around the concession stand in the Pavilion. I did occasionally write parking tickets.

Municipal Pavilion at Center Lake Beach

Center Lake Beach

I also had to drive over to Pike Lake every day to walk the beach area there. Pike Lake Park was where the kids in high school liked to go to make-out on dates—I may or may not have done that a few times myself.

William R. Van Osdol, MD

One summer when I was working at the park, while Susie was recuperating from her neck injury, she very generously let me drive her yellow and white 1957 Ford Fairlane convertible. That car was a beauty, and I loved driving it that summer.

The concession stand at the Center Lake Pavilion was run by Charles and Edna Beanblossom and their granddaughter Sandy Heath. The Beanblossoms also owned a grocery at Little Chapman Lake near our cottages.

Little David Conley, whose sister Sue Conley also worked at the concession stand, was my sidekick when I made my rounds in the park. David liked to pretend that I was Sheriff Andy and he was Deputy Barney.

I tried to eat only from the four food groups when I was a park policeman. Those four food groups were powdered, glazed, jelly, and chocolate frosted doughnuts.

Once I saw a man at the beach with red eyes and I said to him, "You must be drunk, your eyes are red." He said to me, "You must have been eating doughnuts, your eyes are glazed."

The first ticket I wrote was to a man who was illegally crossing the street. The man's name happened to be J. Walker. When I gave him his ticket, the man said, "That's fine with me."

My supervisors when I was a park policeman were Officer Han Kufs and Officer Colin Allcars. Sometimes they asked me to help out with police cases. The first case I helped with was when someone stole some weight loss pills from Walter's Drug store, and the suspects were still at large. Another case was when some campers said their tents were missing, and they asked me to canvas the area.

They asked me to help once when two guys stole a calendar. They were arrested and they both got six months. Another case the police wanted my help with was when someone stole all of the toilets in the police station, and the police had nothing to go on. I must say it was uncanny.

A Time of Innocence

When someone stole 100 pairs of underwear from Phillipson's Clothing Store, they asked me to make a brief enquiry. When someone tried to steal a boat at Center Lake, I was able to keep him at bay.

Once when I was patrolling the beach, I came upon a couple making out who didn't have on many clothes. I told them sternly to put all their clothes back on, and I gave them some sunscreen that I had with me. They didn't mind putting their clothes back on, but they said they objected to the Copper tone.

I also worked one summer at Rodeheaver's Music Publishing Company in Winona Lake, cleaning the place after hours. Rodeheaver's was the world's largest publishing house of gospel music.

I worked one summer at the Wagon Wheel Playhouse for Mrs. Petrie, my speech teacher. I thought I might want to be an actor someday. My job was to help find props for the shows.

I never acted in a play when I worked there, but once my foot was in a cast.

Another summer I worked as a model at the Winona School of Photography in Winona Lake. It was the same photography school where Mom had modeled when she was in high school.

I took the job as a model because at the time it flashed through my mind that I wanted to take a shot at photography. Although I thought I might be a good photographer and it would be a snap by enlarge, I shuttered to think that I might lose my focus and not click at taking photos. So I began to have negative thoughts about it. I finally said, "Although I used to Leica the idea of being a photographer, I have developed other interests."

William R. Van Osdol, MD

Portrait at Winona School of Photography

Chapter 44: My Grandparents

Chester and Inez Bolinger were my Mom's parents and my grandparents. We called them Pappy and Mamaw and we loved them dearly.

Chester and Inez Bolinger

I never knew my other grandparents, Ernest Fleming Van Osdol and Pearl Wheeler Van Osdol—my Daddy's parents.

Pearl and Ernest Van Osdol

Mamaw was a well-known artist. She had an art studio for her oil paintings and ceramics wherever they lived. Mamaw and Pappy's house always smelled so good, like Mamaw's oil paints.

Mamaw in her art studio

Some of Mamaw's ceramics

I really loved the orange chiffon cake that Mamaw made.

Mamaw had two Siamese cats that she named Ming and Ming Too.

I had a feline I should name this memoir after those cats and call it "A Tail of Two Kitties," but I knew I would get the

A Time of Innocence

Dickens if I did that, just like when I once made someone a martini and forgot to put in an Oliver Twist.

When Mamaw and Pappy lived on Columbia Street, we often walked there after school and stayed until Daddy picked us up after work.

We didn't have a television in our house, so when we visited Mamaw and Pappy, we liked to watch soap operas such as *The Edge of Night, The Secret Storm,* and *As the World Turns.*

Pappy was a good carpenter. He made many of the wooden frames for Mamaw's paintings and furniture for her art studio.

"Margie's Alley" (painting by Inez Bolinger)

One of my favorite paintings by Mamaw was called "Margie's Alley." She painted it before I was born, when our family lived on Union Street. The painting portrayed an alley behind our house there, with an old barn, hollyhocks, trees, and a winding path. The painting won prizes wherever it was exhibited.[73]

The painting "Margie's Alley" is now lovingly displayed above the fireplace in our home.

Once I drove Mamaw to Fort Wayne to see her eye doctor. As I drove around the hospital several times looking for a parking space, I noticed that the only parking spaces left said, "Reserved for Doctors."

That was the day I made a momentous decision—I was going to be a doctor. That way, when I went to the hospital I would always have a place to park.

I finally did find a good place to park that day, right in front of a sign that said, "Fine for Parking." The policeman who gave me a ticket was not very understanding.

One day when Mamaw was holding my hands, she lovingly said to me, "Billy, you have the hands of a doctor." I took that to heart in later years.

Pappy had an old gray Plymouth coupe, and he sometimes drove us all downtown and bought us each a bottle of pop. We loved it when Pappy showed us everything that he carried around in his pockets, including an old billfold, twine, coins, photos, a bus ticket, a pocket watch, a handkerchief, a pocket knife, and wood for whittling.

I loved carving wood, too, when I was a whittle boy.

Before I was born, Mamaw and Pappy had a dry goods store, called Bolinger's Dry Goods, in downtown Warsaw on South Buffalo Street. They lost their store during the Great Depression.

Chapter 45: My Aunts, Uncles, and Cousins

Edith and Russell Bolinger were our aunt and uncle. Uncle Russy was one of Mommy's brothers. We called them Aunt Ede and Uncle Russy and we loved them both. They lived in town, not far from the Sacred Heart Church. Uncle Russy and Aunt Ede always came by our house for our birthdays and holidays, and sometimes they stayed for dinner.

Uncle Russy and Aunt Ede.

I always remembered that once at dinner, Aunt Ede asked Uncle Russy, "Do you want a roll?" He said, "Sure, I'll roll with you anytime!" We did not know quite what to think of that at the time.

Uncle Russy sang "Ave Maria" and "The Rosary" at our Mommy's wedding. He had an incredible singing voice, and we loved it whenever he would perform "Ave Maria" for us at family get-togethers.

Uncle Russy was in the Navy during World War II, but he never talked much about that. After the war, he worked at the Power King Tool Corporation in Warsaw.

(L-R) Susan Jane, Uncle Russy, Tommy, and Sally Jo

Uncle Russy and Aunt Ede would buy a new Buick every year or two, and we always looked forward to seeing their shiny new car when they would come to visit.

Aunt Ede worked at the Lake City Bank as a teller for many years. She was gentle, fun-loving, and always kind to us.

And you can take that to the bank!

Lake City Bank souvenir

A Time of Innocence

Mamie and Chester Bolinger were also our aunt and uncle, and we called them Aunt Mamie and Uncle Chetty. Uncle Chetty was the other of Mom's two brothers. Their children were Cy and Ebby. We didn't get to see any of them very often because they lived out of town.

Aunt Mamie and Uncle Chetty

Our other cousins were the Kiefers, who lived in Elwood. Aunt Sarah, who was Mamaw's sister, and Uncle John had five children: Gretchen, Marg (Sister Mark), Ted, Jerry, and Marqueena (Queenie). At times they came to Warsaw to visit us.[74]

Uncle John and Aunt Sarah Kiefer

(L-R) Jerry Kiefer, me, Tom, Aunt Sarah, Margie (in front), Tony, Mary Pat (in front), Uncle John, Bob Kiefer, and John Kiefer in front of our house

(L-R) Margie, me, Mary Pat, Aunt Sarah, Sister Mark, Kathy Kiefer, and Mamaw

A Time of Innocence

My dear godmother, Queenie, was a loving, kind, and gracious woman with a wonderful sense of humor and a ready smile. She was given the name Queen from her parents' love of Mary the Queen, Mother of God. Indeed, Queenie spent her life shining God's love on everyone she met.

William R. Van Osdol, MD

Chapter 46: My Parents in Early Years

Our Daddy, Cortes Dean Van Osdol, was born on September 14, 1903, in Aurora, Indiana. When he was seven years old, his parents moved to Warsaw, where Daddy was raised and attended Warsaw High School.

Daddy and his mother

Daddy was the athletic editor of the high school yearbook, the *Tiger*; sports editor of the *Junior* newspaper; president of the Public Speaking Club; and class secretary. He also played on the basketball team his senior year.[75,76]

Daddy on basketball team   Daddy in senior year of high school

In the senior class will, the Tiger yearbook states, "I, Dean Van Osdol, will my pretty dimples to the junior girls, as a remembrance of me."[77] Also, on a page entitled, "That Ye May Know Them," it lists these responses from Dean Van Osdol:

> Ambition: Go to DePauw
> Adores: Ruth
> Hates: Street cars
> Lacks: Small change
> Feels: With fingers [78]

Now do you understand where I got my sense of humor?

Daddy graduated from Warsaw High School in 1922.

He then went on to DePauw University, where he studied journalism. While at DePauw, he was on the *Mirage* yearbook staff, was the sports writer for the DePauw newspaper, and was on the bowling team. He belonged to the Sigma Delta Chi journalism fraternity and was a writer for the *Yellow Crab*, a humor magazine sponsored by Sigma Delta Chi. Daddy also belonged to the Delta Kappa Epsilon social fraternity.[79]

I learned to be a prankster from Daddy. We loved to hear his stories about putting itching powder in the beds of his fraternity brothers at DePauw. He also told us about the time he pranked one of his professors by posting a notice in the local newspaper requesting that manure be delivered and dumped onto the professor's front yard.

You are probably thinking, "Manure telling some good stories."

Daddy at DePauw   Daddy at dental school

After he graduated from DePauw in 1926, he worked for a while as a sports writer for the *Indianapolis Star*.

Daddy entered dental school at Indiana University in Indianapolis in 1928. He belonged to the Xi Psi Phi honorary fraternity and graduated from dental school in 1934.[80]

Our Mom, Marjorie Louise Bolinger, was born on May 23, 1913, in Warsaw, Indiana. She was sometimes called "Margie Lou" by Mamaw, and later was usually called "Marge" or "Margie." She and her brothers Chet and Russell first lived in Winona Lake; later they moved to Warsaw, on Lake Street (which was on Center Lake).

Mom in younger years   Mom in senior year of high school

Mom attended Warsaw High School. She played basketball for two years, was senior class vice-president, and was on the Athletic Committee, Red Cross Committee, and Reception Committee.[81,82]

In the class will, the *Tiger* yearbook notes, "I, Marjorie Bolinger, do will my love for college fellows to Mildred Mellencamp."[83] Mom graduated from high school in 1931.

Mom was a natural beauty. In fact, there was a time when she was thinking about going to Hollywood. She modeled for the Winona School of Photography and two clothing stores in Warsaw, and she also considered going to modeling school in Chicago.

Mom when she was a model

Mom loved to dance and spent many nights at Tippecanoe Lake (Tippy) Dance Hall. When she was a junior in high school, she was voted Miss Tippecanoe in a beauty contest at the dance hall. She was supposed to go to Indianapolis to compete in the Miss Indiana pageant, but she decided not to go because she was extremely shy and was afraid to be alone in a big city.

Tippy Dance Hall

A Time of Innocence

Mom attended Indiana University in 1931. When she was a student there, she met Hoagy Carmichael, the famous songwriter, singer, and actor. Hoagy performed at student dances, and Mom loved to go to the Sigma Chi fraternity house to listen to his music and sit on the piano bench next to him.

Hoagy Carmichael

At times another musician would sub for Hoagy, but he was not the hero that Hoagy was, no bun intended.

Mom had to drop out of school after one semester after Mamaw and Pappy lost their dry goods store in the Great Depression.

During the next year, 1932, many important historic events occurred. The Great Depression spread world-wide; Al Capone was sent to prison; Amelia Earhart became the first woman to fly solo across the Atlantic; Mahatma Gandhi went on a hunger strike; Cole Porter wrote his hit song, "Night and Day"; Franklin D. Roosevelt was elected President in a landslide; the first Tarzan movie was released; and the atom was split.

William R. Van Osdol, MD

It was also the year in which the Yankees and Cubs played in the World Series and the Yankees won in four straight games. It was during that series that Babe Ruth famously called his shot in Wrigley Field. In the fifth inning with the game tied, he took a called strike, then he pointed to the center field bleachers. He took another strike and again pointed to center field. On the next pitch, he hit a towering home run that landed deep in the center field bleachers—right where he had pointed.

From my perspective, though, nothing was more momentous in the year 1932 than Mom and Daddy meeting each other for the first time. They were introduced at a soda fountain in a drug store in downtown Warsaw by Mom's brothers, who later became our Uncle Russy and Uncle Chetty.

Daddy was called "Cort" at the time, and Mom was quite taken by him. They began dating, and later she called him "Dean." She always said that Daddy was, "The man of my dreams."

Mom was very beautiful and Daddy was very handsome. They looked like movie stars together.

Mom

Daddy

A Time of Innocence

After Daddy graduated from dental school, he worked in Tiffin, Ohio, for six months and then moved back to Warsaw to practice dentistry.

Daddy's Ohio dental license

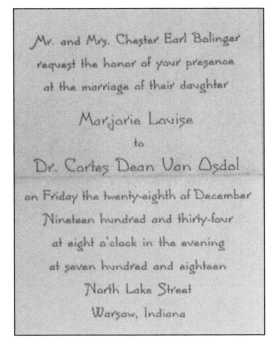

Wedding invitation

William R. Van Osdol, MD

Mom and Daddy were married in Warsaw on December 28, 1934, at Mamaw and Pappy's home on Lake Street.

Mom in wedding gown

Chapter 47: My Parents in Later Years

Daddy said that he was always lonely growing up as an only child. So he wanted a large family, and Mom did, too. Our family joyously grew over the years to seven children: Sara Joan (Sally Jo), Susan Jane (Susie), Thomas Dean (Tommy), me—William Russell (Billy), John Anthony (Tony), Mary Patricia (Mary Pat), and Margaret Ellen (Margie).

Mommy, Daddy, and Sally Jo in Dillsboro, Indiana, in 1937

(L-R) Tommy, Mommy, Susan Jane, Daddy, and Sally Jo in 1941

(L-R) Me, Susan Jane, Tommy, and Sally Jo in 1943

(L-R) Susan Jane, Tony, Daddy, Sally Jo, Mommy, me, and Tommy in 1945

(L-R) Tom, Margie, Susie, Sally Jo, me, Tony, and Mary Pat in 1953

A Time of Innocence

Mom had a journal in which she kept all our family records, including writing down many of the humorous things we said when we were growing up (see Appendix E).

She was an ardent bridge player when she was younger and often let her bridge club meet at our home.

Mom's favorite singer was Ruth Etting, some of whose most popular songs were "Shine on Harvest Moon," "Button Up Your Overcoat," and "Exactly Like You."

Of course, Mom's favorite composer/singer was Hoagy Carmichael. Some of the most popular songs that he wrote were "Stardust," "Georgia on My Mind," and "The Nearness of You."

Her favorite song later in life was "What a Wonderful World," by Louis Armstrong.

When we were ill, Mom would make us milk toast, and it always made us feel better. She also made the best meat loaf, mashed potatoes, scalloped potatoes, bean soup, baked beans, potato soup, potato salad, sloppy Joes, pumpkin pie, rhubarb pie, and peanut butter cookies.

I still have many of her recipes (see Appendix B).

I especially liked Mom's home-made noodles and chuck roast.

When I eat out, I like to bring home some of my pasta because I figure a penne saved is a penne earned. Sometimes I forget that I've left it in the oven, though, and I have learned that those who forget the pasta are condemned to reheat it.

Once there was a butcher named Chuck; while working on a roast, he backed into the meat grinder and got a little behind in his work. That's how we got ground Chuck.

With seven children, there was always a lot of laundry. At first we had a Maytag wringer washer that had to be rolled over to the sink in the kitchen to use it; we would then hang our clothes on the clothesline in the backyard to dry. Later we had both a washer and dryer in the new room.

We got free glasses, as well as dinnerware with a wheat pattern, inside each box of Duz laundry detergent, and a free towel or washcloth in Breeze detergent.

Duz detergent

Mom usually had someone help her do the laundry. We dropped it off once a week at Naomi Snell's house and later at Mrs. Mitterling's house.

It Duz Cheer you up if you are not Tide down by doing laundry All day.

Mom generally wanted us all to take our baths on Saturday night. In the summertime after we had played outside all day, as well as when we were older, we took baths more often.

Mom was soft-spoken, gentle, kind-hearted, and beautiful inside and out. She loved us all unconditionally and liked to call us her "seven precious jewels." We could not have had a better mother.

When Mom and Dad would go out for an evening together, they liked to go to the 30 Club restaurant on Highway 30, east of Warsaw.

A Time of Innocence

30 Club restaurant

Mom and Dad had many good friends. One was Jim Rippey. We liked to talk about him because he would eat fish with the bones still in them. We thought that was just amazing, and that he should be in *Ripley's Believe it or Not*.

Rusty and Jane Valentine were also close friends of our parents, and they often came to our house to visit. They would usually bring their boys, Mike and Pat, who were also our friends. One year all the Valentines went with us to Wildwood Resort in Michigan.

During the summers, we sometimes drove up to Klinger Lake in Michigan to visit Charlie Lamb, a good friend of our parents, and go fishing and swimming.

Klinger Lake. (L-R) Tom, Tony, me, and Mary Pat

Lake Maxinkuckee. (L-R) Exchange student, Dr. George Henricks, David Henricks (in back), Sally Jo, Tom, Tony, Mrs. Henricks, Susan Jane, me, and Mary Pat

30 Club restaurant

Mom and Dad had many good friends. One was Jim Rippey. We liked to talk about him because he would eat fish with the bones still in them. We thought that was just amazing, and that he should be in *Ripley's Believe it or Not*.

Rusty and Jane Valentine were also close friends of our parents, and they often came to our house to visit. They would usually bring their boys, Mike and Pat, who were also our friends. One year all the Valentines went with us to Wildwood Resort in Michigan.

During the summers, we sometimes drove up to Klinger Lake in Michigan to visit Charlie Lamb, a good friend of our parents, and go fishing and swimming.

Klinger Lake. (L-R) Tom, Tony, me, and Mary Pat

Lake Maxinkuckee. (L-R) Exchange student, Dr. George Henricks, David Henricks (in back), Sally Jo, Tom, Tony, Mrs. Henricks, Susan Jane, me, and Mary Pat

A Time of Innocence

Sometimes we would visit another friend of our parents, Dr. George Henricks, who lived on Lake Maxinkuckee in Culver, Indiana. Once we watched the famous Black Horse Troop there.

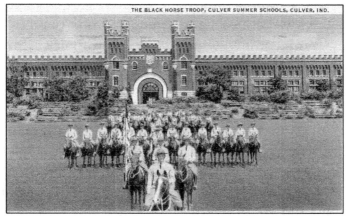

Black Horse Troop

Other close friends of our parents included the Bartols and Stewart Knox. Mr. Bartol once gave us a whole box of arrowheads and other wonderful Indian artifacts.

Indian artifacts given to us by Mr. Bartol

When my brother Tommy was two years old, Stewart Knox gave him a carpenter set. He also engraved Tommy's name on his knife. When we were older, Stewart Knox built us a little green rowboat that we took fishing.

The Fagalys were also good friends of our parents. Sally Jo, Susan Jane, and Tommy often played with their children, Patty and Billy.[84]

Daddy always went to church with us, even before he was baptized in 1949. His baptismal name was Michael, and his confirmation name was Paul. He became a very devout Catholic and was in the men's club, the Holy Name Society, at church.

Our Daddy was always our hero. We never heard him say an unkind word about anyone. He was loving, funny, and unassuming, and we all wanted to be just like him. We were all extremely proud when he was honored as the Father of the Year in Warsaw in 1957.

The article about this began, "Dr. C. Dean Van Osdol, of Route 2, Warsaw, well-known local dentist, is a rich man—rich in the sense that he has put first things first in his life. By so doing he has been blessed. Morally upright, he is respected by his neighbors and business associates. A good father, he has the love of his wife and sons and daughters. Devout in his faith, serenity marks his path."[85]

The article ended, "The Van Osdols are a close-knit family. They worship together, work together, play together, share one another's problems, and most of all, they laugh together. Rich? Yes, Dr. Van Osdol is a rich man."[86]

A Time of Innocence

Father of the Year newspaper article (1957)

Daddy loved bowling. He belonged to the American Bowling Congress, and his team competed in national bowling tournaments. We liked to wear the American Bowling Congress shirts that he would bring home for us from these tournaments.

Daddy (far right) on his bowling team

It is hard to pin down when our Dad first started bowling, but he found that bowling in his spare time was right down his alley.

Before he quit smoking, Daddy usually smoked Raleigh cigarettes. He saved the redeemable coupons that came with each pack.

Raleigh cigarettes

Daddy's pipe tobacco

A Time of Innocence

Many bowlers, though, preferred Lucky Strikes.

Daddy also smoked a pipe for a few years. He used Willoughby Taylor pipe tobacco.

Put that in your pipe and smoke it!

Daddy's favorite singer was Bing Crosby. Some of Bing's most popular songs were "White Christmas," "You Must Have Been a Beautiful Baby," and "Pennies from Heaven."

When Daddy would tuck us into bed, he would say, "Goodnight sweetheart, sleep tight, don't let the bedbugs bite, and don't take any wooden nickels!"

Daddy outside his office on Center Street

We loved to hear Daddy tell the story about a patient who needed a dental plate. Daddy had just received a sample of a new plate that was guaranteed not to break. Daddy showed its indestructible quality by throwing it against the wall. He placed it on the floor and pointed out that you could even jump on it, and it wouldn't break. He then proceeded to jump on it—and the dental plate broke to pieces. Daddy said he felt a little foolish, but the patient still bought the plate, because he said he didn't plan to jump on it.[87]

Daddy really thought he was telling the tooth, the whole tooth, and nothing but the tooth.

Dear Daddy died unexpectedly in 1960 while watching me play in a high school basketball game in the Armory. It seemed like our whole world fell apart, and we were all terribly shaken and downhearted; we missed Daddy so much, and it was all just too sudden.

I always remembered the kindness of our basketball coach, John Stauffer, when he took me aside after the game to explain what had happened. Carl Burt, our superintendent, came out to our house that night to talk to our Mom and to comfort us, as well.

Our dear Mom was heartbroken and overcome with sorrow. Her grief over the loss of our Daddy and the love of her life never seemed to end. It was the price of her eternal love for him.

Mom and Daddy could not have been better parents, and they could not have loved us more. They were wonderful role models, showing us by example how to live our lives—to be kind, honest, loving, courteous, and respectful—and to be devout Catholics.

We were tremendously blessed to have our dear Mom and Daddy for so many years, even though Daddy left us way too soon. We will always miss them, love them dearly, and be forever grateful to them for shaping our lives and giving us the world.

A Time of Innocence

Chapter 48: My Sisters

Sara Joan and Susan Jane were born when my parents lived on Union Street, near downtown Warsaw. They grew up there until I came along, then we all moved into our new home in the woods at the edge of Warsaw.

Sarah Joan, whom we called Sally Jo, was the oldest child in our family, and we all admired and loved her. She had a heart of gold and was always a wonderful role model for us as we were growing up.

Sally Jo in early years

Once when Sally Jo was 12, she was jabbering away at the dinner table. She finally stopped to catch her breath and Susan Jane said, "Sold to the American!"

One day when I was apparently joking about something at the dining room table, which I did on occasion, Sally Jo said to me, "Billy, can't you be serious about anything?"

Sally Jo and Susan Jane both had wonderful senses of humor. Once when we were coming home from church in the car, Sally Jo said, "Daddy, hurry up. It's taking a week to get home!" to which Susan Jane added, "Daddy, you had better get another Sunday paper!"

Sally Jo sang in the choir at Sacred Heart Church. Susan Jane tried out for the choir, too, but they told her she needed to go home and practice.

Sally Jo and Susan Jane both took tap dancing lessons and had recitals; both also took guitar lessons and wrote poetry. They both had many dolls, and their favorite was named Jackie.

Susan Jane also played the accordion.

Accordion to whom you asked, most people said that Susan Jane was a very good accordion player.

Sally's favorite songs were "Mockingbird Hill," "Over the Rainbow," and "Alexander's Ragtime Band." Her favorite singers were Patti Page, Andy Williams, Bing Crosby, and the folk group Peter, Paul, and Mary.

Sally was very popular in school. She had several boyfriends including Ray Heiman, Richard Campbell, and Ian Ross, but Sally never seemed to be very serious about any of them.

Sally in high school

A Time of Innocence

Some of Sally's best friends were Leota Harmon, Mary Ann Long, and Norma Schwierking.[88] Darcy Stouder was also her close friend. One year Darcy went to Klinger Lake with us. Her father was a podiatrist on Center Street in Warsaw.

You should always put your best foot forward when you go to see a foot doctor because you want to get off on the right foot, especially if you want him to heel you. But you don't want to see a podiatrist if he is your arch-enemy or he might add insoles to injury. You don't want to drag your feet or get cold feet thinking about going to a podiatrist, either, because they will know that something is afoot.

Lastly, if you look like a duck and walk like a duck, you probably have webbed toes—you should see a quack doctor and not a foot doctor for that.

One summer when Sally was in high school, she worked at the Flagpole; she also sometimes worked as a babysitter.

When she was growing up, Sally wanted to be a nun, and she never changed her mind. After graduating from Warsaw High School in 1954, she entered St. Mary's Convent at Notre Dame, and her name became Sister Philip Neri. Later on we just called her Sister Sara or Sister Sally.

Sister Sara made the world a better place with her tireless teaching and her work with the poor and disadvantaged. She touched many lives with her kindness, love, and selflessness.

Sister Phillip Neri

Sister Sara has written more than a thousand poems and is also quite accomplished at writing haiku. She has written about 400 haiku, haiku-style, or free-form haiku poems.

I could be out of order for saying this, but I think that being a nun could be habit-forming.

Susan Jane in grade school

A Time of Innocence

Susan Jane, later called Susie, was one year younger than Sally Jo. Susie was a gift to everyone she knew. She seemed to have a light inside her that made people better by just being around her.

When Susie was in junior high, her boyfriends included Roger Fellows, Charlie Ker, and Jack Evans. Susie had crushes on many boys in high school, but her only true boyfriend was Kent Adams.

Susie's closest girlfriends in junior high and high school were Mary Beth and Jo Ellen Hartman (cousins), Lynn Menzie, and Annie Steele.[89]

Susie loved horses. She had a pony that we rented for one summer, named Judy. Then our parents bought Susie her own horse, which she named Gypsy. Later she was given another horse named Lady. We kept both Gypsy and Lady at Helsers's farm, not far from our house.

(L-R) Sally Jo and Susan Jane (on horse Judy), Tommy, Mamaw, and me in our front yard

(L-R) Susan Jane, Gypsy, Mary Pat, Tony, Tommy, and me

It was just equestrian of time before Susan Jane got her own horse. Then she got another horse, but that was a horse of a different color. She liked to ride those horses every day, rein or shine. A Gallup poll showed that Susan Jane's favorite hobby was riding her horses. We never bought her another horse, though, because we didn't want to saddle her with too much responsibility. She sometimes liked to read books by the French philosopher René Descarte—you could say she was putting Descarte before the horse.

Once one of her horses walked into a bar. The bartender asked, "Hay, why the long face?"

I once had a horse named Mayo, because Mayo neighs. I also had a horse with purple reins that I called Prince.

Sometimes we went over to nearby Sensibaugh's farm so that Susan Jane could ride their horse. I told Mom that their horse, named Molly, was mean. When Mom asked me why, I said, "Because she stuck her tongue out at me!"

Susan Jane also had a nice collection of horse statues.

A Time of Innocence

Susan Jane's collection of horse statues

When it came to collecting horse statues, Susan Jane was not horsing around, and you could not rein in her unbridled enthusiasm. Hay, it took her months, neigh years, to complete the collection, and she didn't slow down collecting one bit. I got that straight from the horse's mouth. No, she was not foaling around collecting those horse statues. Yes, I know, some of these horse puns are really lame.

Many people gave her horse statues, sometimes on the spur of the moment, and she would not refuse any of them, manely because she would not look a gift horse in the mouth. She liked to stay up late and play with her horse statues, but Mom would say to her, "Whoa, Susan Jane! Hold your horses and don't stirrup any trouble! It is pasture bedtime, and you need to hit the hay or you might have night mares!"

Susie's favorite songs were "Don't Fence Me In," "Manana," and "Swinging on a Star."[90] Her favorite singers were Frank Sinatra, Bing Crosby, and Patti Page.[91] She also liked the Four Freshmen and went to one of their performances at the Elks Club.

Susie's first job was working at the Flagpole Frozen Custard stand. It became a family legend when a customer once ordered "Five dogs with relish!" and Susie thought the customer had said, "Five dollars' worth of relish!"

Joe Johnson, the owner of the Flagpole, could see Susie was in a pickle, and he didn't relish having to tell her she had the order wrong.

Susie in high school

Susie liked to go to the Tippy Dance Hall when she was in high school. Once she got to hear Louis Armstrong when his band played there. Duke Ellington also performed at the Tippy Dance Hall.

After Susie graduated from Warsaw High School in 1955, she decided to become a registered nurse and went away for training at St. Joseph Hospital in Fort Wayne.

She was engaged to Kent Adams for about a year when she was in nursing school. Later she had another boyfriend, Carl Nadeau, who was from Canada. We wrote another radio script about Canada being on fire, just as we had done to Kent Adams. We thought we might use it on Carl sometime when he came over to see Susie, but we wisely decided against it.

A Time of Innocence

My deer, you Ottawa know that if you are driving up in Canada, there are moose roaming all the roads. Racking your brain, going on a wild moose chase, spending doe on Moose Tracks ice cream, or trying to pass the buck will not keep you from hitting a moose. But if you are really worried that you might hit a moose, and you want to save a lot of bucks, then turn your car radio on really loud to one of the Rolling Stones' songs. That will keep you from hitting any moose, because, as you know, "A Rolling Stone gathers no moose."

Moose are usually careful, though, because they know that only two things are certain in a moose's life: death and taxidermy.

Susie met Terry Engeman at a wedding reception, and Terry asked her to dance with him. Susie's first date with Terry was at a bowling alley.

Terry made three strikes at the bowling alley on their first date, but he did not strike out with Susie. In fact, you could say that Terry bowled her over.

Susie and Terry get married

Terry and Susie became soulmates and got married about eighteen months later.

Terry was a kind, gentle, jovial, and humble man. He was a devout Catholic and he dearly loved his family. Music was always his passion.[92]

Terry had a beautiful soul, and everyone loved him. We miss Terry and his music very much.

Tuba honest, I was never very musical. I did play the coronet in school, but I couldn't keep up with the other kids, so I had to have a tooter. I also tried to play the guitar, but I was too high strung.

I played a cello once, but then I lost it. When I was looking for the cello, I heard Lionel Ritchie singing, "Cello: 'Is it me you're looking for?'" At first they didn't have room for another cello in the orchestra, but then they said, "There is always room for Cello." I thought they were pudding me on.

I would be a lyre, though, if I said I didn't love puns about music. Although some of these puns may be way off-bass, I believe life without musical puns would B-flat. I shouldn't toot my own horn or harp about it, but I know the score and try to B-sharp when it comes to writing musical puns. These puns actually cymbalize my love for music. So I hope you have time to reed them and that they woodwind-up note-worthy and measure up. It's not much treble writing musical puns. It takes me only a minuet, and I think with a concerted effort I could try to drum up some business and sell them for a song.

If you don't like my musical puns, you have my symphony, and I will just have to compose myself and face the music. But it would be music to my ears if you changed your tune and said you liked these puns, and there would be no re-percussions.

I know I should stop the music and rest, and that I shouldn't write any more of these puns or metaphors. I am going to duet anyway, and even though you might not believe I have sunk

A Time of Innocence

Solo, Hans down this could be my best pun, so here it is, "Metaphors be with you!"

I really do have to refrain from writing musical puns now, because as soon as I find my Chopin Liszt, I have to run to the music store. But I will be right Bach.

Susie once fell off a horse and severely injured her neck, and we were all devastated with worry about her. She was in a circular electric bed with tongs in her head for six weeks. She never complained though, and always lived up to what our Mom called her—"Sweet Susie."

Mary Patricia, called Mary Pat, was my next oldest sister. She was always a joy to everyone. She could light up a room like a ray of sunshine with her wonderful spirit and captivating smile, and that never changed.

Mary Pat had a great sense of humor, even when she was very young. At 3 ½, when she saw Daddy carrying a watermelon, she exclaimed, "Daddy, you look like you're going bowling!" Tony was carrying a cantaloupe, and she said, "Tony, you look like you're going bowling, too."

When Mary Pat was almost 4, Sally Jo said to her, "Mary Pat, I made your bed." Mary Pat replied, "You did not. Jesus made my bed."

Mary Pat, Margie, and doll in 1954

About the same time, Mary Pat asked Mommy, "How do you talk?" Mommy said, "You just open your mouth and the words come out." Mary Pat said, "I mean, what makes us talk?" Mommy said, "Well, I guess Jesus just made us that way," to which Mary Pat responded, "What did he do, just wind us up?"

Mary Pat and Margie liked to play school together, and Mary Pat played the teacher. Mary Pat's favorite doll was Sharon.

Mary Pat loved playing wheelbarrow baseball with us. We called her Gil Hodges when she played. Gil Hodges, who played for the Brooklyn Dodgers, was one of our favorite baseball players. Mary Pat was very good at baseball, and she wanted to play for the Fort Wayne Daisies baseball team when she grew up.

Mary Pat contracted polio when she was about 7 and became paralyzed. We were all overcome with worry and sadness, but Mary Pat never complained. She always kept her positive, joyful attitude, and she never lost her beautiful smile. It had to be frightening for her, though, especially when she was in the iron lung, and it had to be extremely difficult for her to accept her sudden disability.

The schools then were not wheelchair-accessible. Mary Pat had a teacher, Mrs. Shoemaker, who came to our house for several

First day of school. (L-R) Margie, Mary Pat, and Tony

years; then she was schooled for three years at home through an intercom. She was finally able to attend the new wheelchair-accessible high school for her last three years of school.

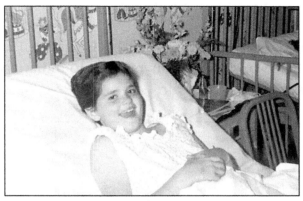

Mary Pat in Shriner's Hospital in Chicago

Mary Pat at her desk at home

We all came together and helped Mary Pat as much as we could by encouraging her, carrying her, and helping with her wheelchair. I often gave her physical therapy on our dining room table.

To paraphrase the famous line from the movie *Boys Town*, whenever I got to carry Mary Pat, I very much felt that "She ain't heavy—she's my sister."

Some of Mary Pat's favorite singers were Elvis Presley, Ricky Nelson, and Johnny Cash. Her favorite song was "I Want to Hold Your Hand" by the Beatles.

I used to know a lot of puns about the Beatles, but that was Yesterday.

Mary Pat's closest friend in school was Genyce Plummer. One year Mary Pat, Margie, and Genyce went to Indianapolis to see a Beatles concert at the State Fair.

Mary Pat in high school

When Mary Pat was in high school, she worked at Harvey's Dime Store. The owners of the store, Mr. and Mrs. Harvey, were very kind to Mary Pat then, and for many years after that.

After Mary Pat graduated from Warsaw High School, she attended Marian College in Indianapolis. Because that school was not wheelchair-accessible, she transferred to the University of Illinois, where she graduated.

A Time of Innocence

While attending the University of Illinois, Mary Pat met and fell in love with Ernie Hodge, the handsome, generous, witty, and kind-hearted man who would become the love of her life.

Mary Pat and Ernie get married

Margie on top of refrigerator

Margaret Ellen, called Margie, was the youngest in our family. When she was born, she became "Daddy's girl," just as Mary Pat had been when she was the youngest. She was the best little sister anyone could ask for. She had a winsome smile and a gentle, loving heart, and she could brighten any room.

Once when Margie was 3, she had just had a bath and was sitting in the living room wrapped in a towel. Susie's then boyfriend, Kent Adams, came to the house for a date with Susie. Margie finally pushed the towel off, and Dad said, "Oh, Margie, let me cover you up—Kent might see you." Margie said, "Too late— he already saw me."

When Margie was about 6, I asked her if she knew what the opposite of "sweet" was, and she didn't know. So I asked, "What is the name of the baseball player—you know, his first name is Hank....Hank.... what is it?" "Oh, yes," said Margie, "Hank Sauer." "Ok," I said, "That's right. So then what's the opposite of sweet?" Margie answered, "Hank!"

Two of her teachers that Margie remembered fondly at Sacred Heart grade school were Mrs. Snellenberger and Miss Summer. In middle school, her favorite teacher was Mr. Clyde Conley. Margie's closest friends in school were Marcia Miller, Janet Robertson, and Phil Bowman.

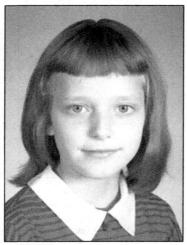

Margie in grade school

A Time of Innocence

One of Margie's summer jobs was working at the lunch and soda fountain counter in Judd's Drug Store. She also worked for a while at the telephone company and at the YMCA

Margie liked to play canasta, played on a softball team, and was quite a good artist. She may have inherited more of Mamaw's artistic talents than any of us.

Margie in high school

Margie's favorite songs were "Sound of Silence" "How Sweet It Is to Be Loved by You," and "Tupelo Honey."[93] Her favorite singers were Simon & Garfunkel, James Taylor, and Van Morrison.[94]

After Margie graduated from Warsaw High School, she attended Indiana University in Bloomington. That was during the era of the hippie counterculture, which included psychedelic drugs, streakers, long hair, peace signs, flower girls, rock festivals, and singers such as the Grateful Dead, The Who, and Bob Dylan.

Margie went to the rock musical *Hair* during that time. **She nude it would be a good musical, and I hair she really liked it.**

Margie and Max get married

Margie met Max Brown one day at IU when they were playing softball. Max was tall, handsome, and athletic, had a sexy southern accent, and sported a distinctive beard, all of which duly impressed young Margie. They began seeing each other every day, and two years later she married Max—the affable, gentle, and kind-hearted man of her dreams—in Beck Chapel on the Indiana University campus.

A Time of Innocence

Margie met Max when they were playing softball, and at first they just touched base with each other. Max didn't know if he could get to first base with Margie, or if she was out of his league. He didn't know if she would tell him to take a walk, if she would throw him a curve ball, if he would strike out with her, or how it would wind-up. Max liked to sing when he played softball, but he did not have good pitch.

Max did not balk, though. He was on the ball, and right off the bat he knew Margie was a big catch and that he wanted to steal her heart. He no longer wanted to play the field, and didn't want to let things slide or make an error, so he stepped up to the plate, made a shortstop at the phone booth, and called to ask her out (although first he had to cleanup). Their first date was to see the Star Wars movie, *The Umpire Strikes Back*.

Later, Max decided to swing for the fence, and out of left field he gave Margie a diamond. Margie was ecstatic, although she would have preferred getting a diamond ring instead of a softball diamond. Still, Max was a big hit with her, and she knew then that she had knocked it out of the park and was batting a thousand with him.

For his part, Max knew that there would be no more singles clubs, double dates, or triple shots, because he had hit a home run when he met Margie, and it would be a whole new ball game after that.

They decided to get married, and they served bunt cake at their wedding. Some of the orchestra members at their wedding had too much to drink; they played Beethoven's Ninth, and the bassists were loaded when it was the bottom of the ninth.

It would seam that I have covered all the bases with this story, but if not, that's just the way the ball bounces!

William R. Van Osdol, MD

Chapter 49: My Brothers

Thomas Dean, called Tommy, was born when our parents lived on Union Street. He moved with our family to our new home when he was two years old.

Tommy was quite a fisherman at a very early age. One day when he was only five years old, he and Daddy were trolling with a green flatfish lure on Pike Lake, and Tommy was nearly yanked out of the boat when he hooked a giant channel catfish. When they were finally able to pull in the fish, Daddy put it on a stringer and dropped it over the side of the boat. Then the huge fish, which was said to be probably the largest catfish ever caught on the lake, broke the stringer and swam away. Tommy told everyone that the catfish was as long as an oar.

Believe it oar not!

Tommy loved basketball. In his early years, he carried his basketball around with him, took it to school, and even took it to bed.

Tom in 7th grade

A Time of Innocence

Tom loved baseball and played in Little League. He also played Pony League and American Legion baseball when he was older.

The first year Tom played Little League, he was on the All-Star team. He was also the batting champion, with an unbelievable batting average of .622. Some of the other kids that played with Tom on the All-Star team that first year were Jay Clutter, Chuck Yeager, and Jerry Aylor.[95] The All-Star team got beat in their first Little League tournament game in Hobart, Indiana.

Tom swinging bat in backyard

Sometimes during lunch hour in junior high, Tom would run to the Humpty Dumpty restaurant in downtown Warsaw; quickly eat his standing order of a cheeseburger, fries, and milk shake; then race to the Boys Club at the high school to play basketball with some friends, who would later play with him on the high school team. He would then run back to junior high before classes started again.

When Tom was on the high school basketball team, he was one of their best players. Warsaw won the sectional tournament two years in a row. Some of his teammates were Bob Koedyker, Max Bolinger, and Charlie Hollar.[96]

Tom was also on the high school baseball team, football team (freshman year), and cross-country team.

Tom on freshman football team

Tom loved to hunt and fish, and he collected Mercury dimes and baseball cards. He always seemed to be making something. Once he made a movie about Abbott and Costello entitled "Abbott and Costello Meet Atlas," using drawings on a small roll of paper and a shoe box.

One time when he was older, Tom decided to practice shooting his shotgun before rabbit hunting season. He had Margie run through the woods pulling a tin can behind her on a long rope, while Tom shot at the can with his shotgun. Tom thought that would give him good practice for shooting rabbits. (I'm not sure how Tom ever talked Margie into that…)

When Tom went rabbit hunting, it was hare today and gone tomorrow.

I didn't go hunting much as a kid, although I did go rabbit, pheasant, and quail hunting when I was a little older.

It always seemed to be hit-and-miss when I went hunting.

Tom also liked to perform magic and put on magic shows. He got many of his tricks from the book *Dunninger's Magic Tricks*.

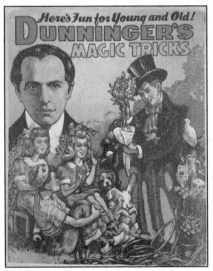

Book of magic tricks

I once knew a magician who never took the magician's exam because he thought there would be too many trick questions. He liked to saw people in half—I saw it with my own eyes. After he sawed someone in half, he would thank them for being a part of the show, and they would say, "Thank you for halving me." The magician lived with his three half-brothers and three half-sisters.

Tom also liked to play with his Gilbert chemistry set, which he kept on top of his dresser in our bedroom.

Tom and his friend Dean Shively once tried to raise beagles, and they put up a fence for the dogs down in the woods. **They found out that raising beagles was not all that it was cracked pup to be.**

Tom's closest friends in school were Mike Fitzpatrick, Jay Clutter, Dean Shively, Hugh Siefken, Bill Murray, and Dave Castaldi. Tom's favorite songs were "The Green Door," "Sixteen Tons," and "Big Bad John."[97] Some of his favorite singers were Louis Armstrong, Perry Como, and Dean Martin.[98]

Tom would sometimes go out to the Fitzpatricks' house, where they would play in the barn and make tunnels out of hay in the hay loft. Mike Fitzpatrick's sister Kathy was a good friend and classmate of mine.

One time Tom, Mike, and Jerry (who was Mike's brother, and whose nickname was Pick) were playing around in the barn with their pocket knives. Tom and Mike decided to drop their knives straight down while standing, trying to get the blade to land between their toes. Then Pick tried it, and when he dropped his knife, it stuck right in the top of his foot!

We were all very proud of Tom when he was chosen to be an exchange student. He traveled to the Netherlands in the summer between his junior and senior years of high school. He stayed with one Dutch family, the Boegheims, above their family bicycle shop in Gouda, and with another family in a different town. He sailed on the Zuiderzee, traveled to Austria and Germany, and drove on the famous Autobahn highway (no speed limit).

A Time of Innocence

Tom leaving for Holland

When he came back home, Tom brought wooden shoes and some Gouda cheese, and he had wonderful slides of the Netherlands to show everyone.

I would love to go to Holland myself—wooden shoe? The nights are cold there, but the Hollandaise are hot and you never sauce such weather. Still, you have to take the Gouda with the bad. When Tom went out to eat with the family in Holland, they usually wanted to go Dutch.

When Tom was asked how he was Dylan with the many questions that he was asked about windmills, he said, "The Answer, My Friend, is Blowin' in the Wind."

After he had been back home awhile, and everything had settled down and was not so quixotic, he would Don his thinking cap, tilt back in his chair, and say, "Mancha the time, I am a big fan of windmills."

Tom may have wanted to bring home some tulips from Holland, but he would have gotten in Dutch for it. When he finally made it home for Thanksgiving and Christmas, and got to have a plate of our Mom's home cooking, including eggs Benedict, he was excited because, "There's no plates like home for the Hollandaise!"

Tom was senior class president and president of the student council. He was able to negotiate trading Senior Skip Day for having no final senior exams. There were no final senior exams for several years after that, thanks to Tom.

Tom in high school

When their beloved principal, James Whitcomb Riley (named after the famous Indiana poet), passed away during his senior year, Tom was appointed acting school principal for the rest of the year. Tom graduated from high school in 1958.

One of Tom's first summer jobs was working at Clark's Oil gas station in Warsaw. He got really good at pitching quarters to try to land on a crack in the driveway. That was their favorite pastime at the station when they weren't busy.

A Time of Innocence

That was the summer that Tom met Linda Conley.[99] On their first date they went to see the movie, *The Apartment*, starring Jack Lemmon and Shirley MacLaine, at the Lake Theatre.

"Shirley you can't be serious," you say. "I am serious," I say, "and don't call me Shirley!"

We didn't know if it was Linda's engaging charm, her captivating beauty, or her loving and kind heart that took young Tom's breath away and swept him off his feet. Tom soon knew, though, that this was true love, and that they would always be together. They got married two years later.

Tom and Linda get married

It must have been around the Fourth of July when Tom met Linda, because sparks were flying. They starting dating when he was working at Clark's Oil, and fuel get this pun, but oil's well that ends well.

Tom's boss at the Clark's station was Tom Hoover, who was a basketball star when he was in high school in the nearby small town of Mentone, which called itself the "Egg Capital of the World."

Tom Hoover really was a good egg.

My brother Tom also had a job one summer driving a Freezer-Fresh soft serve ice cream truck.

Tom at first thought he wanted to be a tennis player, but the real scoop was that he had a soft serve, so he decided to sell ice cream instead. That was a cool job. In fact it was so cold in his ice cream truck that he was afraid he might come down with a bad case of spumonia. He learned all about ice cream in Sundae School. At first the ice cream kept dripping down the cones, but he was able to lick that problem. Tom was nice to everyone, because he thought they all deserved a fair shake. He always carried an umbrella in his truck in case of sprinkles.

He had to work every day, even on Sundaes. One time his truck broke down because of the rocky road. He drove his ice cream truck so slowly that most people thought he was a Sundae driver. Another time his green ice cream melted, but it was mint to be. He knew he was spending too much money on premium ice cream, so he began having Breyer's remorse.

He once had a customer named Reese who wanted to eat her ice cream cone Witherspoon.

Freezer-Fresh ice cream truck

A Time of Innocence

Another summer, Tom had a job working for an electrician.

Tom was ec-static about working for an electrician, and it was a good outlet for his energy. He also liked the idea that if you need something done, you can call an electrician and they conduit and would always know watt to do.

When he would come ohm late from working for the electrician, his mother would say, "Wire you insulate? I am shocked by your behavior and you are grounded until you learn how to conduct yourself!"

I should have more resistance to writing these puns, but they seem to electrify me, and I have amp-le time to do it. I hope you are not re-volted by them, or that you have a short fuse or are negative about them, because I really get a charge out of writing them.

They told Tom that shorts could be dangerous for electricians, so he never wore shorts to work. He was never shocked by watt they told him because he had kept current about those things.

After Tom graduated from high school, he attended St. Joseph College for two years. He did play on the basketball team his freshman year, as a walk-on late in the season. He played in only one game, but he had his moment of glory when he stole a pass, resulting in the winning basket.

After two years at St. Joseph College, Tom attended Indiana University School of Dentistry in Indianapolis, studying in the same building where our Daddy had learned to be a dentist.

We came from a long line of dentists that included our Daddy, our grandfather Ernest, and our great grandfather Charles. It was not surprising then, when Tom followed in their footsteps and became an incredible dentist.

Growing up, I always thought that I would also become a dentist, like Daddy and Tom. In fact, I signed up for pre-dental courses at Notre Dame. After two years there, when most of my friends were in pre-med,

I decided I wanted to become a physician instead and switched into the pre-med program. After three years at Notre Dame, I attended Indiana University School of Medicine in Indianapolis.

No one could have been a better big brother than Tom. He was wise, kind-hearted, and adventurous, and was much like our Dad in many ways. We all looked up to Tom, and I always wanted to be just like him.

Even today, if I am in a difficult situation and not sure what I should do, I ask myself, "What would Tom do now?"

John Anthony, called Tony, was the youngest of the boys in our family. Tony, Tommy, and I were close in age and played together most of the time in our early years.

(L-R) Tommy, me, and Tony

When Tony was two years old, Daddy said, "Tony, don't you want to go to bed?" Tony said, "No, I went to bed last night." At age 4, Tony said, "I can run faster than Tommy, I can. Sometimes my feet just kick my bottom, I run so fast."

Tony loved to collect postage stamps and baseball cards, read, go fishing, and play chess and board games.

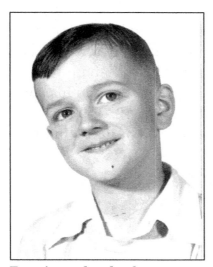
Tony in grade school

Tony and Mary Pat

Tony with the bass he caught at Pleasant Lake in 1956

Tony was a good athlete and played Little League baseball. The first year he played for the Cubs Little League team, he had the best pitching record for his age, with four wins and no losses.

Tony always had a problem with his bowels in his early years. He was badly constipated and Mom would have to give him frequent enemas. He would not come willingly to get the enemas; he would run and hide in the woods, and Mom would have to send Tommy or me out to find him and bring him into the house.

When Mom would ask Tony if he had pooped in his pants, he would say, "No, B. did it." (Tony called me "B.")

Bathroom puns aren't my favorite kind of jokes, but they are #2.

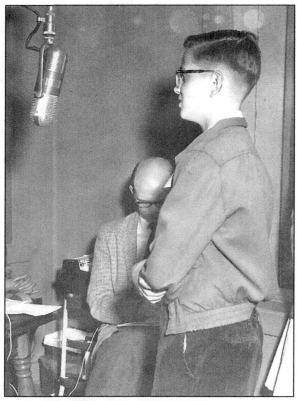

Tony in spelling bee

A Time of Innocence

We were all extremely proud of Tony when he went to Washington, DC, to compete in the National Spelling Bee. Susie and Tony went on the train first so they could visit the sights of interest. Susie was Tony's chaperone. The rest of our family drove there in our car later.

The train ride to Washington was tiring, and after he got there, Tony had to sit down for a spell.

Tony had studied the dictionary in preparation for the spelling bee. He was so smart that it seemed he could spell every word in that book. But he misspelled the word "feral" and finished 13th in the National Spelling Bee.

I read once about someone who actually swallowed a dictionary. He said that was Thesaurus throat he ever had, but after that he was never at a loss for words.

During that trip, Tony and our parents had some other excitement, as well, when they sat next to Senator John F. Kennedy while riding on a tram underneath the Capitol building.

Tony in high school

William R. Van Osdol, MD

Tony's closest friends in high school were Ed Snodgrass and Mike Valentine. His first job was working at Puckett's cafeteria in downtown Warsaw; he worked there several years while he was in high school.

After Tony graduated from high school in 1963, he attended the University of Notre Dame. After graduation, he attended the Indiana University School of Law.

Tommy and I liked to play pranks on Tony in our younger years, but we couldn't have loved him more or been more proud of him. Tony was also a lot like Daddy—smart, kind-hearted, gentle, and loving. And like Daddy, he left us much too soon, and we will love and miss him forever.

Chapter 50: West Wayne and East Wayne

My brothers, sisters, and I all went to West Wayne grade school, which was far over on the other side of town. We had to ride the bus to get there. We were usually the first kids picked up in the morning and the last to be dropped off at home after school. The ride was so long that it sometimes made my bottom "go to sleep." Chauncey Rife was our bus driver, and later it was Mr. Patterson.

West Wayne School. (Photo courtesy of Michelle J. Bormet, *A History of the City of Warsaw, Indiana*)

Sally Jo and Susan Jane in front of our bus

I usually sat in the front seat and saved a seat next to me for my best friend, Eddie Huffer. Eddie was funny, happy-go-lucky, and a loyal friend. Our bus also picked up Billy Huffer, who was one of Tommy's best friends, as well as many other kids we knew.[100,101,102]

Billy and Eddie Huffer

At West Wayne School

A Time of Innocence

I loved my teachers at West Wayne School, including Mary and Bea Riley, Mary Kincaid, Edna McCartney, and Francis Reece (who was also our principal). I was somewhat fearful of Mr. Reece, though, because he had a big paddle in his office that he was known to use if you badly misbehaved.

West Wayne School 1st grade class. I'm in the middle row, third from left. Our teacher was Miss Mary Riley

The first time I got into trouble at West Wayne was in Miss Mary Riley's first grade class. I was banging my feet on the back of the desk in front of me with a distinct rhythm. Miss Riley said, "Whoever the Indian is beating on his drum, please stop!"

William R. Van Osdol, MD

Report cards from West Wayne School

A Time of Innocence

West Wayne had a wonderful little gymnasium with a shiny linoleum floor where I learned to play basketball. There was a cafeteria at one end of the gymnasium, classrooms on both sides, and a stage at the other end. During recess and after lunch, I usually played basketball in the gym or kickball outside, walked around the school on the cinder track, raced other kids, and played on the jungle gym, merry-go-round, and swings.

Holding basketball

There was only one kid in my class at West Wayne who could run faster than I could, and that was Maynard Merica—also one of my good friends.

I had to go to the principal's office only once at West Wayne. That was when I got into a fight on the playground with Denny Blue, who was actually one of my best friends.

That may have been the only time I was paddled by the principal. Someone must have told on me. No one likes a paddle tale!

We liked to take our squirt guns to school, and we had some really great squirt gun fights. But if we got caught, the squirt guns would be taken away, and we'd never get them back. I noticed that one of my teachers had nearly a whole drawer full of confiscated squirt guns.

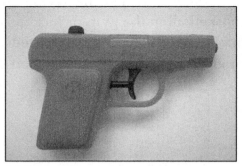

1950s squirt gun

Although I liked my classmates in grade school, some especially good friends were Larry Brubaker, John Bilby, and Mike Munson.[103] Some girls who were my friends at that time were Linda DePoy, Alice Ann Manrow, and Sally Webb.[104]

4th grade class at West Wayne School

A Time of Innocence

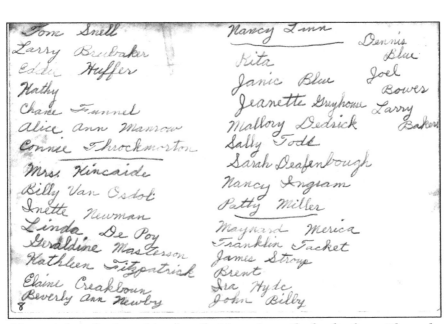

Names of students and teacher that I wrote on the back of our 4th grade class photo

6th grade class at West Wayne School. That's me in the middle row, on the far left.

We often had oatmeal cookies for lunch at West Wayne. It seemed that most of the other kids in my classroom didn't like them. They all knew I loved oatmeal cookies, so most of them gave their cookies to me. I collected a big stack of those cookies on my desk and devoured them all in no time.

That would bake my day! Sometimes I would get into trouble because of all the pieces of cookies left on my desk, but I would tell my teacher that was just the way the cookie crumbles.

In the fourth grade at West Wayne School, we had a server in the cafeteria named Ginger. If you asked her for more than one cookie, it would make Ginger Snap at you. She was one tough cookie.

One of my classmates, who will go unnamed to protect his identity, became a legend in the seventh grade when we were on a field trip to Chicago to see the Field Museum of Natural History and the Museum of Science and Industry. When our bus stopped at a rest stop along the way, the aforementioned classmate decided to leave and hitched a ride all the way to California.

There was a small grocery store near West Wayne School, across Highway 15. I used to go there sometimes during the lunch hour to buy root beer barrels, Bazooka bubble gum, and Necco wafers.

When I was in the seventh grade, I rode the bus first to West Wayne School, then I transferred to another bus and rode to East Wayne School. East Wayne was located in the town of Winona Lake. My teacher there was Mr. Sands, and the principal was Mr. Cox.

A Time of Innocence

East Wayne School (Photo courtesy of Michelle J. Bormet, *A History of the City of Warsaw, Indiana*)

7th grade class at East Wayne School. I'm second from the right in the front row.

When I was at East Wayne, I took a class in agriculture and learned all about farming, including crops, cows, pigs, chickens, and tractors. I liked the class so much that, for a while, I thought I might want to be a farmer.

I thought that if I was a farmer, I could be outstanding in my field.

I heard about a farmer who had a girlfriend, but she left him for a tractor salesman. She sent him a John Deere letter.

I loved playing basketball in the little gymnasium at East Wayne. Sometimes we had track meets; I won ribbons once for both the shot put and the 220 yard dash.

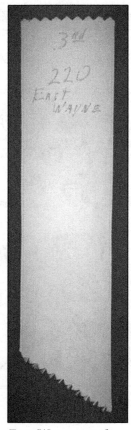

East Wayne track ribbon

A Time of Innocence

Once I tried out for the chorus at East Wayne. I had to sing "Home, Home on the Range." They told me I needed to go home and practice; that was the first time I really knew that I simply could not carry a tune.

Chapter 51: Junior High School

For eighth and ninth grades I attended Junior High School, located downtown next to Center Ward School and the Armory.

Junior High School

I admired and respected all of my wonderful teachers there, including Mrs. Anderson, who taught math; Mr. Stafford, who taught Latin and liked to ride his bicycle to school; Coach Lichtenwalter, who was our physical education teacher; and Mr. Bryan.[105]

Mr. Bryan taught us shop, and we called him "Coffee Cup Bryan," because he often carried a coffee cup around when we were working on our projects. I made a maple bookcase in Mr. Bryan's shop class.

We still use that bookcase downstairs to hold bar glasses.

A Time of Innocence

8th and 9th grades

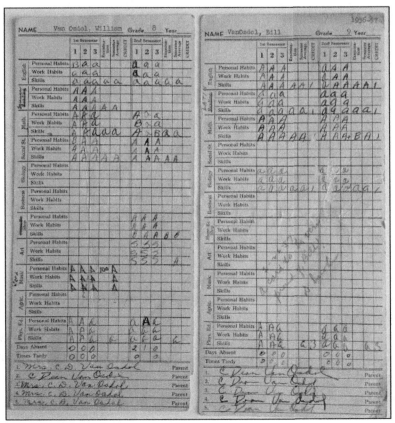

8th and 9th grade report cards

I remember playing tug-of-war in junior high gym class. They threw me off the team because I wasn't pulling my weight.

I was on the track and field team in junior high. The events I usually entered were the broad jump and hurdles.

Track and field ribbons

I worried a lot that I could not jump the hurdles, but I finally got over that.

I also played on the basketball teams in the eighth and ninth grades. Some players on the ninth grade basketball team with me were Dave Delp, Denny Blue, Bud Zolman, and Bill Grow.[106] Our coach was Bill Goshert, and our team manager was Steve

Cartwright. The ninth grade cheerleaders were Tim Snyder, Barb Hauth, Susie Mollenhour, and Sally Webb.

That's me kneeling on the far left

Bob "Bubba" Phillips, Dave "Hammer" Delp, John "Faker" Foresman, Bill "Hoovie" Hoover, Don "Pitti" Pittenger, a few other guys, and I sometimes liked to play phone pranks during the lunch hour.

Pitti and Hammer in junior high

We would find a pay phone, go through the phone book, and call someone randomly. One of us would tell the person who answered that they could win a million dollars if they could name the song we were going to sing. Then Faker would sing, "Beware, beware, beware." He sang just those words over and over again. Still, few people could name the song, which, of course, was supposed to be "Beware."

We played other phone pranks, as well. Sometimes we would call a gas station and ask if they carried Ethyl. When they said "Yes," we'd say, "Isn't she heavy?" and hang up.

Or we would call a tobacco store and ask, "Do you have Prince Albert (a brand of tobacco) in a can?" They'd say, "Yes," and we'd yell, "Let him out! He can't breathe!"

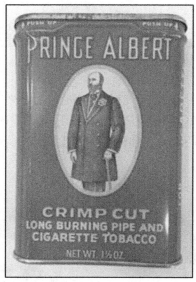

Prince Albert in a can

One year Bubba, Hammer, and some other friends in junior high decided to play a prank by replacing the Kotex with Hershey bars in the vending machine in the girl's locker room. Bubba and Hammer always seemed to be the ringleaders in any mischief.

A Time of Innocence

Bubba in junior high

They must have put Hershey bars with almonds in the vending machine, because someone heard one of the girls say, "Aw, Nuts!" But those Hershey bars can cost you an almond a leg, and you wouldn't believe the cashew had to shell out to some nut named Hazel, who worked at the candy store. The guys didn't know what would be a Goodbar to use, because they wanted to get a lot of Snickers from everyone. They even thought about using candy bars with raisins in them, because they thought that would be raisin the bar.

Hershey bars with almonds

It was named the "Great Kotex Caper," and the principal called several of the culprits into his office in confection with the whole affair. It was the best prank ever, bar none.

My first date was with Mallory Dederick, when I was in junior high. I took her to a dance at the Armory. I had to ask Susie to show me how to dance just before I went.

On my first date

Chapter 52: High School

I attended Warsaw High School. I admired and respected all of my incredible teachers, especially Esther Pfleiderer, (who taught math), Mildred Petrie (who taught speech and directed our class plays), and Mamie Braddock (who taught English and also wrote poetry).[107]

Warsaw High School

One time Mrs. Braddock called on me in class to name two pronouns. I hadn't been paying much attention, so I said, "Who, me?"

Our principals in high school were Dane Snoke, James Whitcomb Riley, and Bill Davis. Our beloved superintendent was Carl Burt.

I also had great sports coaches including John Stauffer (basketball and cross country), Dave Burke (basketball and cross country), and Howard Bock (baseball).[108]

All of my teachers, principals, and coaches were dedicated and served as extraordinary role models. They were kind, patient, and inspiring. Each of them helped make me the person I am today, and I will always be grateful to every one of them.

I was on our speech team and gave humorous and dramatic interpretations in tournaments. My humorous interpretations included "Green Pastures" and "Barefoot Boy with Cheek." One of my dramatic interpretations was "Afraid of the Dark." I liked to practice my interpretations at home for Margie and Mary Pat.

Giving declamation in speech tournament

In my junior year in high school, I was in the play *Stardust*. During my senior year, I acted in *The Matchmaker*.[109]

A Time of Innocence

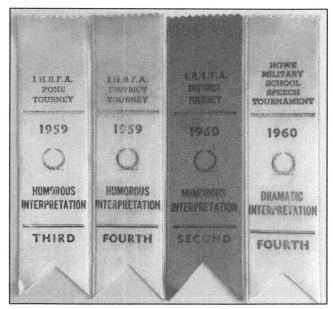

Speech tournament ribbons

Junior class play *Stardust*. Me and Betsy Steele

William R. Van Osdol, MD

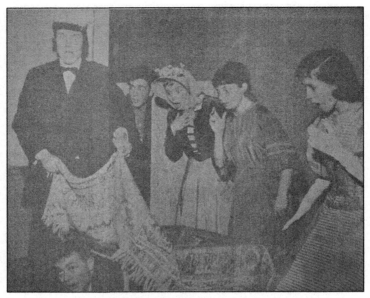

Senior class play *The Matchmaker*. (L-R) Me, Richard Beers, Betsy Steele, Katie Eggers, and Pauline Elliott

Of course, the desire to prank followed me from junior high to high school. I was not very proud of one particular prank, which I called "Hot Lips," perhaps because it did not have a good ending. It was my first date with a girl I liked during my sophomore year. To protect the innocent, she shall go unnamed here. We were going to a dance, and I decided that I wanted to impress my friends. So before the dance, just for this occasion, I ordered a lip stamp from the *Johnson Smith Catalog of Novelties*. On the way to the dance, while riding in the back seat with my date, I secretly put red lipstick, which I had borrowed from one of my sisters, on the lip stamp. Then I stamped the lipstick all over my face and neck making it look as if my date had been madly kissing me.

I hadn't exactly considered how my date would feel about this. When we got out of the car, she took one look at me and was furious. She told me in no uncertain terms that I needed to immediately remove all of the lipstick before we went into the dance. Furthermore, she said that I should not bother to ever ask her out again!

My date also told me that I had to keep my lips sealed about the whole thing, and that I had better not give her any lip about it!

I was mostly disappointed, though, that my friends never got to see the lipstick all over my face, because I was sure they would have been quite jealous.

During my junior year in high school, on the day we were having our school pictures taken, my glasses were broken and I had them taped together. I didn't really want to have my picture taken with my glasses looking that way. I asked one of my friends, Tom Snell, who was standing in line next to me, if I could borrow his glasses for my picture. He kindly let me do it. That was how my school pictures that year showed me wearing black horn-rimmed glasses for the first time.

Junior year of high school

William R. Van Osdol, MD

When I got my school pictures back during my senior year, one of my classmates said the pictures made me look sexy. I rather naively blurted back, "Don't say I look 'sexy,' it's just not proper to say that word."

Senior year of high school

I probably didn't like improper fractions either.

I was on the junior varsity basketball team my sophomore year, and the varsity the next two years. My nickname on the basketball teams was "Skyhawk." Some of my teammates when I was a senior were Jim Aker, Dave Delp, Les Konkle, and Billy Grow.[110] Our coach was John Stauffer, and the assistant coach was Dave Burke. Our team managers were Bubba and Hoovie.

A Time of Innocence

Warsaw basketball team my senior year. That's me sitting on far left

During one basketball game, when Bubba was upset with a referee's call, he threw his clipboard and it slid all the way across the court.

The Armory, where we played basketball games

When our team practiced after school in the Armory, I loved it when I looked up at the balcony and saw that Daddy had walked over after work to watch me practice.

In making the basketball team, I realized one of my childhood dreams. That dream was to experience the excitement of running onto the Armory court with the team in our white, home warm-up uniforms; shooting layups while the crowd stood and cheered; and hearing the band play the stirring Warsaw High School fight song:

"Warsaw High, Warsaw High,
Warsaw High, we're all for you,
We will fight, fight,
With all our might, might,
For the victory, we'll win for you.
Never shaken, till foe is taken,
The fighting battle, we're tried and true,
Warsaw High, Warsaw High,
Warsaw High, we're all for you!"

Old Elks building

A Time of Innocence

After the basketball games, we usually went to the sock hops held in the old Elks building downtown. We danced in our socks to the "The Stroll," slow danced to songs such as "Twilight Time," "Dream Lover," and "I'm Sorry," and fast danced doing the jitterbug to "Johnny B. Goode," "At the Hop," and "Peggy Sue."[111]

We also had dances in the school gymnasium during lunch hours. Usually, though, it seemed that the girls did most of the dancing, while the boys just stood around and watched.

I played on the high school baseball team for three years. One year my brother Tom and I were on the team together. Some of my teammates were Dave Delp, Jim Aker, and Don Pittenger. Sometimes after baseball practice, Jim Aker would drive some of us out to the Flagpole in his 1959 red Olds.

While I didn't play football on the high school team, some of my good friends who did were Don Pittenger, Kevin Smyth, Jim Aker, and Dave Delp.[112]

I missed my chance to play on the football team. The coach wanted me to go out for the team and be the quarterback. I was really excited about it and said, "I'll pass." The coach said, "OK, but you had your chance."

It was during our senior year, on the night before our last football game with our arch rival Columbia City, when about twelve guys in three cars led by Kevin "Smitty" Smyth drove over to Columbia City. They had cans of orange and black paint, and plans to paint our rival's goalposts. Smitty often seemed to be involved when there was ever any mischief.

When they got there and began running up the road to reach the football field, they didn't notice the cable stretched across the road in the darkness. Smitty, who was running ahead of the others, ran straight into the cable, which knocked him down. He hit his head and was knocked out for a few seconds. But the rest of the guys went ahead as planned and painted the goalposts orange and black, Warsaw's school colors.

Of course, the officials at Columbia City knew it had to be Warsaw students who had painted the goalposts, so the next day they notified our principal. Principal Davis then began questioning the usual suspects. Larry Baker, who had been one of the guys involved, at first tried to take all the blame for the prank, but Smitty came forward and confessed that he had been the leader.

The only punishment Smitty was given was that he had to go to Columbia City and apologize on stage to the whole school. When he spoke to the students there, he mentioned that one of the reasons our guys had done it was to get back at Columbia City for painting Warsaw's goalposts maroon and yellow—Columbia City's school colors—four years earlier.

Smitty, who became my roommate at Notre Dame the following year, became a legend in his own time for being the instigator of the "Great Goalpost Escapade."

Kevin "Smitty" Smyth

I ran on the cross country team for three years during football seasons. One year Tom and I were both on the cross country team.

A Time of Innocence

We had to run from the high school to the fairgrounds after school to practice. I liked picking and eating the pears off the pear trees lining the railroad tracks on the way to the fairgrounds.

I wasn't going to eat the pears off the trees, but my teammates told me I should do it, and I gave in to pear pressure.

Some of my classmates who were on the cross country team were Mike Munson, Mark Cosgrove, Monte Reece, and Jack Bradbury. Dale Benson was also on the team with me for two years and was one of our best runners.

I had crushes on a lot of girls in school including Linda Truman, Linda DePoy, Betsy Steele, and Jean Kelley, but I never dated any of them. My somewhat steady girlfriends in high school were Judy Philapy, Alice Ann Manrow, and Mary Lou Rose.

I liked all of my high school classmates. Some of my closest friends were Bob Phillips, Bill Hoover, Jim Aker, Dave Delp, Don Pittenger, John Bruner, Mark Cosgrove, and Bud Zolman.[113]

Bud Zolman

Bud was a kind-hearted and loyal friend. He was so cool with his black leather jacket, pegged pants, and slicked-back ducktail haircut. He was our own "Fonzie" (from *Happy Days*), and like "The Fonz" he could be your defender and protector.

We had some really fantastic cheerleaders in high school including Susie Mollenhour, Sally Webb, Lana Pinkerton, Barb Hauth, and Jenny Bartlemay.

I was an alternate delegate to Boys' State one year and went down to Indiana University in Bloomington to participate.

Somehow I was voted class president in my senior year. I was just following in Tom's footsteps, though, because he had also been senior class president.

Senior class officers: Susie Mollenhour on left, me in back, Bob Phillips in front, and Judy Philapy on right

A Time of Innocence

Crowning homecoming queen, Patty Mulcahy

Somehow or other I was also voted senior prom king, once again following in my brother Tom's footsteps.

Me and Sally Webb reign as prom king and queen

On Saturday nights in the summertime, my friends and I would often go dancing at the Tippy Dance Hall on Tippecanoe Lake. It was the same place that our Mom loved to go dancing when she was in high school, and where she was voted Miss Tippecanoe.

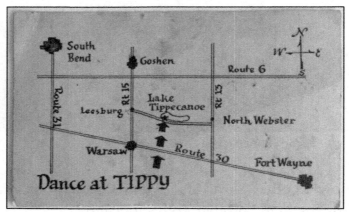

Directions to Tippy Dance Hall

Attractions at Tippy Dance Hall in 1958

On the way to Tippy Dance Hall, we would sometimes stop to eat at the Barbee Hotel on Big Barbee Lake. The Barbee Hotel was famous because in earlier years gangsters such as Al Capone, John

A Time of Innocence

Dillinger, and Baby Face Nelson hung out there. They wanted to get away from Chicago while gang wars were going on.[114]

Barbee Hotel

Movie stars such as Clark Gable, Carol Lombard, and Rita Hayworth also liked to stay at the Barbee Hotel. It was said that Clark Gable and Carol Lombard even honeymooned in a log cabin near the hotel.[115]

Today, the rumors are that the Barbee Hotel is haunted. Some people say they still smell the smoke from Al Capone's cigars in room 301 where he stayed.[116]

One year I recited Lincoln's Gettysburg Address in a Memorial Day ceremony at the Oakwood Cemetery.

Here's a little history lesson for you...Abraham Lincoln had some friends named Paul and Mary Getty. They had a pet bird that liked to wear little dresses. One day Lincoln delivered the Getty's bird a dress.

On a scale of 1-5, that pun gets a four score.

William R. Van Osdol, MD

Receiving an American Legion award

While in high school, I was fortunate to win the Elk's award for baseball, as well as an American Legion award.

I graduated from Warsaw High School in 1960.

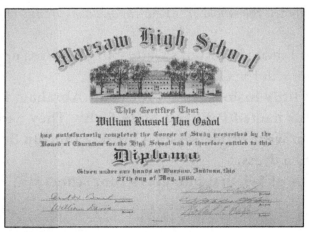

Warsaw High School diploma

A Time of Innocence

Chapter 53: Loss of Innocence

Dear reader, can you remember when you were a kid, how thrilling it was when you took your last ride of the summer on the roller coaster at the county fair?

Can you also recall watching fireworks on the Fourth of July, and how excited you were when the spectacular grand finale lit up the sky?

You are about to experience those same thrills and that same excitement when you read this grand finale of puns and the end of my story. So buckle up, it's going to be a bumpy ride...

When we were seniors, our basketball team got to go down to Indianapolis to watch the state basketball finals at Butler Fieldhouse. We all looked forward to having a great adventure in the big city.

We stayed at the Continental Hotel downtown on Friday night, before the ball games on Saturday. After dropping water balloons out the window for a while, we decided we wanted to go out on the town and have some real fun.

Fox Theatre. (Photo credit Bass Photo Co. Collection, Indiana Historical Society)

It was probably Bubba, one of the usual instigators of any of our mischief, who came up with the idea that we should all go to the Fox Burlesque Theatre.

I was seriously nervous and not at all sure I wanted to go with my friends to a burlesque show. I remembered those words of Charles Atlas, the famous bodybuilder, who said, "Live clean, think clean, and don't go to burlesque shows."

I thought about what I had learned in catechism. Would it be just a venial sin if I went to the burlesque show, or could it even be a <u>mortal</u> sin?

In one significant way, I was not unlike my Mom. As I recounted earlier, when she was my age she was so shy that she wouldn't even go to Indianapolis to participate in the Miss Indiana contest.

Still, I thought I was probably old enough to go to the burlesque show, and maybe I could just keep my eyes closed—and anyway, it would probably be just a venial sin.

As we all hesitantly walked through the door of the Fox Burlesque Theatre that night, no doubt everyone in the place thought we had just come in from the farm, because we all looked quite naïve and so green that the cows could eat us.

They didn't even ask our ages when we entered. We just paid to get in, and then they gave each of us a box of Cracker Jacks.

As we all nervously walked down the dark, narrow aisle to find our seats, I couldn't help but wonder if there might be bigger surprises on the stage than there were in those Cracker Jacks boxes. It wasn't long until I found out.

Bubba sat in the front row so he could prop up his leg, which was in a cast. Bill Hoover sat next to Bubba. The rest of us, including Dave Delp, Jim Aker, and I, sat in the row behind them, where we probably thought we were a little safer and less conspicuous.

Then the show we had been nervously awaiting finally started.

A Time of Innocence

The strippers on stage that night were the Cuban Bombshell, Pink Champagne, and the famous burlesque queen Rose LaRose. There were also comics who told risqué jokes between the strippers' acts.

The famous Rose LaRose

I had finally decided that I really should open my eyes. We all sat there wide-eyed as we watched the strippers, the likes of which none of us had ever seen before. About all we could hear during the show, though, was Bubba's uproarious, howling laughter from the front row reverberating throughout the theater.

As I was finishing this story and eating some delicious Godiva chocolates, it occurred to me that I was not unlike the famous legend Lady Godiva, who said, as she was nearing the end of her naked horseback ride, "I am now drawing near my clothes."

However, you must endure a little more pun-ishment before my story actually ends.

We had all kept abreast of the times, so we knew that the Fox Burlesque Theatre was located in a strip mall. I am going to give you only the bare facts about what happened next.

When I walked through that door at the burlesque theater, I noticed right away that because it was a strip joint, there was no wallpaper on the walls. I also thought about how we used to booby trap our bedroom door to keep our sisters out. Could there be a booby trap waiting for us inside?

There were no strippers on the stage when we first sat down, so I thought, "No nudes is good nudes."

I decided to open my eyes when the show started because I didn't want people to think I was too clothes-minded.

Remembering the names of the strippers is like a walk down mammary lane. Strippers could barely make a living, and when they were out of work, they had no acts to grind. I do remember that one of the strippers was an electrician, and she had to strip to make ends meet.

I took some photos of the show, but I couldn't get them developed because they were over-exposed.

As we sat there in stark surprise, we were all looking a little pale and pastie. At first we couldn't bare to watch, but as the show went on, the strippers became more appeeling.

Later, as we were sitting there watching the show and eating chicken strips that we had gotten in the buff-et line, the police suddenly burst in and raided the theater. Most of the strippers barely got away, but it was a clothes call and one got busted. I think she nude that might happen, especially because she had not re-nude her stripper's license. She was acquitted, though, because they could not pin the wrap on her. In the local papers, there was very little coverage of the strippers.

After the show was over, as I slowly made my way out of the Fox Theatre, I knew that in some inexplicable way I had changed, that I had grown up and come of age that night.

Yes, I knew for certain that fateful night had been the end of my age of innocence.

And that, my dear friends, is the naked truth.

It is now my respunsibility to tell any of my readers who are either camping or swimming with dolphins, that for all in tents and porpoises, this memoir has come to an end.

A Time of Innocence

Appendix A: Radio Broadcast

Hello, Ladies and Gentlemen. This is Frank Frick with the *64 Cents Question* show, the radio quiz program in which the contestant wins two cents for the first question and can keep going, doubling the total each time until he wins the grand prize of 64 cents. If he wishes, he may stop after any correct answer and keep what he has won, because if he chooses to go all the way and should miss one, he loses all he has made. The contestant has five seconds for each question. Now a word from our sponsor.

Ladies and Gentlemen: Does your cereal always stay crisp and crunchy when you eat it? If it does, you should buy Creamy Slurps, the cereal that always stay refreshingly soggy and sloppy. Buy some from your favorite store today.

Now it's time for the 64 Cents Question show. Our contestant tonight is Tony Van Osdol. Tony, where are you from? Warsaw? Why that seems familiar somehow. Well, Tony, are you ready for your first question, for two cents? You will have five seconds. Bill, are you ready with the stop watch?

Here we go. Fill in the missing word. He laughs _____ who laughs last.

Why is the period of late July to early September called "the dog days"?

How many squares are there on a chess board?

Who wrote Rip Van Winkle?

When Mr. Truman became the president, what office was next in line to succeed him?

Ok, here we go for the jackpot 64-cents question: The male is "testador;" what is the female called?

Appendix B: Favorite Recipes

VANILLA ICE CREAM

6 medium eggs
2 cups + 6 T. sugar
1 pint half and half
1 ½ pint whipping cream
1 quart whole milk
2 ¼ T. real vanilla
¼ tsp. salt

In large bowl beat eggs. Then mix in sugar and beat. Then beat in milk, whipping cream, half and half, vanilla and salt. Pour into freezer container and then freeze.

ESCALLOPED POTATOES

6 potatoes
Salt
Pepper
Flour
1 stick of utter
3 cups milk

Peel potatoes and slice thinly. Then layer in buttered casserole dish. Sprinkle layer with salt, pepper, flour, and dots of butter. Continue layers of potatoes and for each layer add salt, pepper, flour, and butter. Heat milk and pour over potatoes. Bake at 350^0 uncovered for 1 hour 15 minutes.

A Time of Innocence

TOM AND JERRYS

12 eggs
12 teaspoons powdered sugar
12 jiggers Bourbon whiskey
Nutmeg

Separate egg yolks from whites and beat each in separate bowls. When eggs are beaten, combine them in a large bowl, and stir gently. Next stir in powdered sugar and add whiskey. Use soup ladle and fill tea cups only half full. Then pour enough very hot water to fill cup nearly full. Sprinkle a dash of nutmeg on top.

PEANUT BUTTER COOKIES

1 cup or 2 sticks oleo or butter
1 cup white sugar
1 cup (packed) brown sugar
1 cup peanut butter
1 tsp. vanilla
3 beaten eggs
2 tsp. baking soda
2 tsp. water
3 cups flour

Mix butter, sugars, peanut butter and vanilla. Then add eggs and mix. Add baking soda dissolved in water. Mix and gradually add flour. Mixture will be very thick. Roll into walnut-sized balls size and place on greased cookie pan 1 inch apart. Make some balls the size of marbles for smaller children. Mash down with fork. Bake at 375^0 for 8-10 minutes. Makes 5-6 dozen depending on size of ball.

MILK TOAST

Two slices bread
1 cup milk
Butter
Sugar (white or brown)
Dash of nutmeg

Toast bread. Spread butter on toast and sprinkle with sugar. Put toast in large soup bowl. Heat one cup of milk and pour over toast. Can put a dash of nutmeg on top, if desired.

Appendix C: The Ballad of Johnny Sands

There was a man named Johnny Sands
Who married Betty Hague,
Although she had both gold and land,
She proved a terrible plague.

Says he, "My love, I'll drown myself,
The river runs below."
Says she, "Pray do, you silly elf—
I wished it long ago."

"For fear that I might courage lack
And try to save my life,
Pray tie my hands behind my back."
"I will," replied his wife.

She tied his hands behind his back,
And when securely done,
"Pray now, my love, stand on the brink
While I prepare the run."

So down the hill, his loving bride
She ran with all her force
To push him in. He stepped aside
And she fell in, of course.

Then splashing, dashing like a fish,
"Oh, save me, Johnny Sands!"
"I can't my dear, though much I wish,
For you have tied my hands."

Appendix D: Thanksgiving Day at the Kiefers

Over the hill and thru the wood
To Kiefer's house we go.
Our Chevrolet
Will be our sleigh
As we leave our bungalow.

Across the river and thru the wood
Oh, how the sun does shine.
We all feel so cozy,
And Baby gets dozy
As over the roads we wind.

Down the valley and thru the wood
Past fields where corn-stalks lay.
The wheels seem to hum,
"Here we come, here we come,"
For John and Sarah's day.

Over the hills and thru the wood
To Sarah and John's chateau.
This is the date
To celebrate
When Sarah wed her beau.

Across the river and thru the wood
To St. Joe's on bended knee.
For Sarah will mention
A prayer of intention
And one for good John D.

A Time of Innocence

Down the valley and thru the wood
To let the children play.
St. Chris will you guide us?
From harm will you hide us?
We fold our hands and pray.

Over the hills and thru the wood
I hope we won't be late.
We seem to go
Extremely slow
It's so very hard to wait.

Across the river and thru the wood
As we glide along the way.
Of turkey we're dreaming
With dressing that's steaming
For this is Thanksgiving Day.

Down the valley and thru the wood
To see Sister Mark we'll roam.
We'll look in the kitchen
And see her eye glisten
For once again she's home.

Over the hills and thru the wood
Thru Kiefer's door we'll file.
There's a birthday 'tis said
For our cousin Ted
So we'll sit and chat awhile.

William R. Van Osdol, MD

Across the river and thru the wood
At Kiefer's house we'll visit.
There are birthdays galore—
Was Jerry's before?
Let's honor them all while we're at it.

Down the valley and thru the wood
Now Kiefer's house we spy.
Hurrah for the fun,
Are the noodles done? Hurrah for the pumpkin pie.

By: Marjorie L. Van Osdol
With apologies to Lydia Maria Child

Appendix E: Excerpts from Mommy's Journal

Billy says, "Goodbye, my Dear," to everyone that's leaving the house.

Billy says, "Member what Chamie Chaus said." (Remember what Santa Claus said—he said you have to let everybody play with your toys.)

Billy says, "Rooks rike a rion but it immit, immit?" (Looks like a lion but it isn't, is it?)

Billy says, "When I grow up, can I be Santa Claus? Oh, no, I don't want to be Santa Claus, 'cause he lives where the bears live."

Billy says, "I'm sorry God, I love you God for everybody else."

Billy says, "I love God, do you?"

Billy, age 5. "I don't ever want to get married. I don't ever want to go to war."

Billy, age 5, "Do you think God loves us as much as we love God?"

Billy, age 8, was taking a bath the night before the first day of school. Billy says, "Oh, boy, I feel like a new man."

Billy, age 9, "This summer is lastin' slow, isn't it Mommy."

Billy, age 11, "Tony, you got to practice up baseball." Tony, "Why?" Billy, "Don't you know you're the last of the 'Great Van Osdols'?"

Mamaw says, "You better turn that teakettle off, it's boiling its head off." Billy says, "I don't see any head, Mamaw."

Billy often asks to say the rosary—if we have said it once, he wants to say it again—he says, "I like to say the rosary."

Billy says, "God, please make Mary Pat hurry and grow up." "Why Billy?" "Because I want to play with her."

Billy says, "Mommy, I don't like these dimples all over my face." I said, "What dimples?" Billy says, "Don't you see 'em? They're all over my nose, 'n over here—and here." I said, "Oh, you mean freckles."

Billy says, "I pray to God not to ever let the world end." "But you know He said it would end someday," I said. Billy says, "Yes, but I don't ever want to go to heaven. I don't want the world to end because I always want to stay home with you and Daddy." "But you won't ever see God." Billy says, "Yes, I will—I see God everywhere but I can't see him. What does God look like?" I said, "Nobody knows till they get to heaven." Billy asks, "Will he look like Daddy? Will he wear glasses, do you suppose?"

Endnotes

1. Gaynor Borade, "Family Life in the 1950s: A Decade of Social and Economic Prosperity," historyplex.com.
2. Harvey Schmidt and Tom Jones, "Try to Remember," 1960.
3. Other parish priests were Father Lothamer and Father John Reddington (from Notre Dame).
4. Other sisters who taught us catechism were Sister Mary Eva, Sister Ann Joachim, and Sister Bertha.
5. *Wikipedia* contributors, "Necedah Shrine," *Wikipedia, The Free Encyclopedia*, accessed July 5, 2019, en.wikipedia.org.
6. Ibid.
7. Ibid.
8. Matthew Kelly, *The Biggest Lie in the History of Christianity*. (North Palm Beach, FL: Blue Sparrow Books, 2018), 35.
9. Mitchell Symons, *That Book of Perfectly Useless Information*. (New York: HarperCollins, 2004), 18.
10. Other favorite card games were old maid, crazy eights, blackjack, and poker.
11. Other favorite board games were Sorry, Password, checkers, and Scrabble.
12. Other favorite cowboys were Red Ryder, Johnny Mack Brown, Monte Hale, Gabby Hayes, Bat Masterson, and the Cisco Kid.
13. Gene Raskin, "Those Were the Days," 1960.
14. Other Cubs players I liked were Toby Atwell, Bob Addis, Frank Baumholtz, Johnny Klippstein, Dee Fondy, Clyde McCullough, Gene Hermanski, Joe Garagiola, Dutch Leonard, Bob Ramazotti, Turk Lown, and Bill Serena.
15. Other favorite baseball players were Jackie Robinson, Bob Feller, Roberto Clemente, Ralph Kiner, Satchel Paige, Pee Wee Reese, Roy Campanella, Whitey Ford, Sandy Koufax, Phil Rizzuto, Harmon Killebrew, Minnie Minoso, and Robin Roberts.

16. Other older favorite Hall of Fame baseball players were Jimmy Foxx, Grover Cleveland Alexander, Cy Young, Tris Speaker, and Walter Johnson.

17. Some of the other players on those first Little League Cubs teams were Dennis Blue, Dick Lesh, Jay Benson, Barry Nieman, Ron Autenreith, Jim Craig, Bill Dederick, Ron Dirck, Ed Joyner, Steve Conley, Johnny Rutherford, Roger Gelbaugh, Jerry Aylor, Nolan Huffer, John Foresman, Jay Clutter, Chuck Yeager, and Larry Koser.

18. Michelle J. Bormet, *A History of the City of Warsaw, Indiana*, Kosciusko County Historical Society (Bourbon, IN: Harmony Visual Communications, 2001), 115.

19. Other favorite professional basketball players were Tom Gola, Neil Johnston, Dolph Schayes, Elgin Baylor, Ed Macauley, Johnny Kerr, Paul Arizin, and Jim Pollard.

20. Other favorite professional football players were Frank Gifford, Norm Van Brocklin, Lou Groza, George Blanda, Sid Luckman, and Doak Walker.

21. Other favorite Notre Dame football players were Jim Morse, Neil Worden, George Haffner, Dick Syzmanski, Frank Varrichione, Art Hunter, and Sam Palumbo.

22. Other professional golfers I liked were Julius Boros, Gary Player, Tommy Bolt, and Cary Middlecoff.

23. Other professional tennis players I liked were Vic Seixas, Ken Rosewall, Lew Hoad, and Frank Sedgman.

24. Other candy I liked included Oh Henry, Milky Way, Three Musketeers, and Chuckles.

25. Other favorite chewing gums were Teaberry, Dentyne, Beech-Nut Spearmint and Wrigley's Juicy Fruit, Spearmint, and Doublemint.

26. Other scatter pins we made were hats, deer, kittens, and seahorses.

27. Alfred Lord Tennyson, *The Charge of the Light Brigade,* 1854.

28. Robert Service, *The Shooting of Dan McGrew*, 1907.

29. Livingston, May, and Foster, "I Tawt I Taw a Puddy Tat," 1950.

30. *Wikipedia* contributors,"Burma Shave," *Wikipedia, The Free Encyclopedia*, accessed July 5, 2019, en.wikipedia.org.

31. Frank Rowsome Jr., *The Verse by the Side of the Road* (New York, NY: Plume, 1979.)

32. Other favorite fishing lures were Rapalas, Jitterbugs, Nip-I-Diddees, Slim Jims, Spoon Plugs, River Runts, and Skitter Baits,

33. Other magazines I read were *The Saturday Evening Post* and *Time*.

34. Other favorite comic strips were *Popeye, Steve Canyon, Kerry Drake, Dr. Morgan, MD,* and *Dennis the Menace.*

35. Other favorite comic books were *Hopalong Cassidy, Gene Autry, Lone Ranger, Roy Rogers, Lassie, Donald Duck, Mighty Mouse, Tarzan, Space Cadets,* and *Dick Tracy.*

36. More favorite radio shows were *The Green Hornet, Sergeant Preston of the Yukon, Tom Corbett Space Cadet, The Adventures of Ozzie and Harriet,* and *The Shadow.*

37. Other favorite boxers were Archie Moore, Sugar Ray Robinson, and Floyd Patterson.

38. More favorite race car drivers were Tony Bettenhausen, Eddie Sachs, Lloyd Ruby, Pat O'Connor, Pat Flaherty, and Jim Rathman.

39. Bormet, *A History of the City of Warsaw*, 137.

40. Other favorite movie actors were Gregory Peck, Cary Grant, Rock Hudson, Marlon Brando, Paul Newman, James Dean, Burt Lancaster, Charlton Heston, James Cagney, Robert Mitchum, and John Wayne. Other favorite movies actresses included Rita Hayworth, Kim Novak, Katherine Hepburn, Ingrid Bergman, Deborah Kerr, Sophia Loren, Ava Gardner, Lauren Bacall, Jane Russell, and Lana Turner.

41. Other favorite movies were *The High and the Mighty, Giant, Cat on a Hot Tin Roof, Rear Window, The African Queen, The Man Who Knew Too Much, Magnificent Obsession, On the Waterfront, The Robe, Maltese Falcon,* and *20,000 Leagues Under the Sea.*

42. Other favorite songs were "Blueberry Hill," "Sixteen Tons," "Till I Waltz Again with You," "Music, Music, Music," "Manana," "The Yellow Rose of Texas," "You, You, You," "This Old House," "You Send Me," "On Top Of Old Smokey," "Ghost Riders in the Sky," "Shrimp Boats," "Born to Lose," "I Get Ideas," and "Mockingbird Hill."

43. Some other favorite older songs were "Buttons and Bows," "I Don't Want to Set the World on Fire," "White Cliffs of Dover," "I'll Be Seeing You," and "Paper Doll."

44. Other favorite silly songs were "Does Your Chewing Gum Lose Its Flavor on the Bedpost Overnight," "Beep! Beep," and "Alley-Oop."

45. More favorite songs we would sing when we were younger were "London Bridge," "Ninety-Nine Bottles of Beer on the Wall" (a bus song), "The Old Gray Mare," "My Bonnie Lies Over the Ocean," "Fifteen Men on a Dead Man's Chest," "Row, Row, Row Your Boat" (a bus or car song), and "She'll Be Coming 'Round the Mountain."

46. Other favorite singers were Ray Charles, Bobby Darin, Pat Boone, Burl Ives, Brenda Lee, Teresa Brewer, Kay Starr, Jo Stafford, Perry Como, Jerry Lee Lewis, Fats Domino, Johnny Ray, Tony Bennett, Tennessee Ernie Ford, Little Richard, Bobby Vinton, Frankie Avalon, Paul Anka, Fabian, Eddie Fisher, and Bing Crosby.

47. Other favorite singing groups were the Lettermen, Four Lads, Four Aces, Kingston Trio, Four Preps, Mills Brothers, Bill Haley and the Comets, Platters, Ray Coniff Singers, and Coasters.

48. Bormet, *A History of the City of Warsaw,* 175.

49. Other favorite nursery rhymes were "Old Mother Hubbard," "Little Jack Horner," "Sing a Song of Sixpence," "Baa Baa Black Sheep," "Little Boy Blue," and "Hickory Dickory Dock."

50. More favorite fairy tales were *Little Red Riding Hood, Sleeping Beauty, Cinderella, Hansel and Gretel, Goldilocks and the Three Bears,* and *The Three Little Pigs.*

51. *Wikipedia* contributors, "Charles Atlas Course," *Wikipedia, The Free Encyclopedia,* accessed July 5, 2019, en.wikipedia.org.

52. Brett and Kate McKay, "The Art of Manliness: Lessons in Manliness from Charles Atlas," posted in 2011, artofmanliness.com.

53. Ibid.

54. *Wikipedia* contributors,"Bosco Chocolate Syrup," *Wikipedia, The Free Encyclopedia,* accessed July 5, 2019, en.wikipedia.org.

55. Ibid.

56. Ibid.

57. *Wikipedia* contributors, "Captain Midnight," *Wikipedia, The Free Encyclopedia,* accessed July 5, 2019, en.wikipedia.org.

58. Other favorite cereals were Grape-Nuts, Rice Krispies, and Corn Flakes.

59. Other Wheaties sports cards I liked were Bob Feller, Sam Snead, George Mikan, Yogi Berra, Bob Lemon, Jack Kramer, Otto Graham, Roy Campanella, and Phil Rizzuto.

60. More prizes from cereal boxes were Hopalong Cassidy Wild West trading cards, Tom Corbett Space Cadet membership cards, Lone Ranger rings, western tin badges, Sky King decoders, Dick Tracy whistles, plastic cars and trucks, and 3-D glasses.

61. Bormet, *A History of the City of Warsaw,* 73.

62. Other rides we liked at the county fair were the caterpillar, Dodgem bumper cars, and the Little Dipper roller coaster.

63. Other favorite games on the midway were throwing darts at balloons, tossing coins, knocking over milk bottles, tossing rings, and shooting basketballs.

64. Other Exhibit baseball cards I liked were Gil Hodges, Hank Aaron, Warren Spahn, Al Dark, Hank Bauer, Enos "Country" Slaughter, and Richie Ashburn.

65. More chalk statues we won were ships, Disney characters including Donald Duck, Pinocchio and Snow White, and Charlie McCarthy.

66. Other Christmas songs I especially liked were "White Christmas," "Deck the Halls," and "I'll Be Home for Christmas."

67. Some other Christmas carols I liked were "Oh, Little Town of Bethlehem," "We Three Kings," "Oh Christmas Tree," "Deck the Halls," "Hark the Herald Angels Sing," and "It Came Upon a Midnight Clear."

68. Michelle J. Bormet, *A History of the City of Warsaw*, 193.

69. Dan Coplen, "A Special Kind of Place: the Flagpole Custard Stand was a Warsaw Icon.," (Warsaw, IN: Kosciusko County Historical Society, 2006).

70. Some of my friends who were in the Koastin' Krates Derby in 1950 (there was no Soap Box Derby from 1941-1951) were Jerry Eaton and Dave Delp, when they were both eight years old. In 1955, other friends in the Soap Box Derby included Billy Grow, Jim Aker, Ted Dobbins, and Dale Benson. In 1956, Dick Adams drove a car that was entered by Bob Phillips. In 1957, Bob Phillips, then age 14, advanced to the local semifinals.

71. Sally Coplen Hogan, *Kosciusko County Soap Box Derby*. (Kosciusko County Historical Society, 2014), 25-78.

72. Dale Benson was one year ahead of me in high school, went to medical school with me, and was in my internship and residency classes at Methodist Hospital in Indianapolis. Later he hired me to work with him for HealthNet, a network of

community health centers in Indianapolis, where I worked for 43 years. Dale has remained a close lifelong friend.

73. Marguerite Sand, "Inez Bolinger," posted in 1956, yesteryear.clunette.com.

74. Our Kiefer cousins included: Queenie and Dick and their children (Kevin, Jerry, John, Beth, Margaret, Shelly, Dave, Kathleen, and Ann); Ted and Ruth and their children (Terry, Bob, John, Marqui, Liz, Kathy, Greg, Steve, Theresa, Tim, and Nick); Jerry and Rita and their children (Mary Sue, Sarah, Patty, Dave, Michaellen, and Chris); and Gretchen and her son, Joey.

75. Warsaw High School yearbook, *Tiger* (Warsaw, IN: Reuben Williams & Sons, 1922), 37.

76. Some of Daddy's other activities in high school were the Glee Club, Cadets, Public Speaking Club, Junior Class Play, Senior Class Play, Latin Club, Spanish Club, Student Council, Junior Red Cross, Science Club, and Alpha Alpha Alpha honorary fraternity.

77. Warsaw High School yearbook, *Tiger*, 1922, 48.

78. Ibid., 135.

79. DePauw University yearbook, *The Mirage of 1926* (Greencastle, IN: DePauw Junior Class, 1926), 50.

80. Indiana University yearbook, *The 1934 Arbutus* (Bloomington, IN: Undergraduates of Indiana University, 1934), 398.

81. Warsaw High School yearbook, *Tiger* (Reuben Williams & Sons; Warsaw, IN, 1931), 17.

82. Some of Mom's other activities in high school were the Operetta, Special Chorus, Glee Club, and Science Club.

83. Warsaw High School yearbook, Tiger, 1931, 54.

84. Other close friends of our parents were Ron Lamb, Harry Hall, and the Steeles, Morgans, and Bashes.

85. Marguerite Sand, "Local Father Is Wealthy Man," *Warsaw Times-Union*. (Warsaw, IN, Reuben Williams & Sons, 1957.)

86. Ibid.

87. Ibid.

88. Other friends of Sally Jo in high school were Patti Sumpter (she rode our bus), Mary Ramsey, and Nettie Nice.

89. Some more of Susan Jane's best friends in school were Carol Eggers, Nadine Heitman, Martha Jo Coplen, Sandra Weirick, and Phyllis Fawley.

90. Some of Susie's other favorite songs were "Rock Around the Clock," "Mack the Knife," "Pistol Packin' Mama," "Four Leaf Clover," "Don't Let the Stars Get in Your Eyes," "Music, Music, Music," and "Sh-Boom."

91. Some of Susie's other favorite singers and bands were Perry Como, Nat King Cole, Glenn Miller, Benny Goodman, Tommy Dorsey, Ella Fitzgerald, Mills Brothers, Johnny Mathis, Jo Stafford, Bobby Darin, Kay Starr, Mario Lanza, Tony Bennett, Teresa Brewer, Johnny Ray, Kingston Trio, Four Freshmen, and Bill Haley and the Comets.

92. Terry loved teaching music. He directed bands in elementary, junior high, and high schools in Fort Wayne and South Bend. He greatly enjoyed performing percussion for the Fort Wayne Philharmonic, South Bend Symphony Orchestra, and South Bend Pops and for musicals in The Round Barn Theatre at Amish Acres in Nappanee, Indiana. Terry had many devoted private students, did church and dance jobs. He also taught percussion at Notre Dame and other colleges.

93. Some of Margie's other favorite songs were "Blowin' In the Wind," "Everything is Beautiful," "Raindrops Keep Falling on My Head," "Born Free," "Summer Breeze," "Let It Be," and "The Dock of the Bay."

94. Some of Margie's other favorite singers were Peter, Paul and Mary, Diana Ross and the Supremes, Moody Blues, Bob Dylan, The Beatles, John Denver, and Cat Stevens.

A Time of Innocence

95. Other Little League All-Stars that year were Bob Holbrook, Larry Shively, Greg Zuck, Mike Ringer, Bill Grubbs, Ronnie Anderson, and Ron Autenreith.

96. Other players on Tom's basketball teams were Lavon Harmon, Art Long, Hugh Siefken, Joe Sensibaugh, and Jim Sumpter.

97. Some of Tom's other favorite songs were "The Yellow Rose of Texas," "It's All in the Game," "That'll Be the Day," "Diana," "Banana Boat Song," "Love Letters in the Sand," "Little Darlin'," "It's Only Make Believe," and "Kisses Sweeter Than Wine."

98. Some of Tom's other favorite singers were Frankie Valli, Tennessee Ernie Ford, Buddy Holly, Pat Boone, Andy Williams, Frank Sinatra, and The Lettermen.

99. Tom and his friend, Dean Shively, were cruising the streets of Warsaw in Dean's Ford convertible one summer during Pioneer Days. Linda was walking alone on the sidewalk carrying a shopping bag. They stopped to talk with her and had a short conversation, then offered to take her home. Linda accepted the ride. Dean wanted Tom to fix him up with Linda, but Tom didn't do that. Instead, Tom called Linda himself and asked her to go out on a date with him.

100. Some other kids who rode on our bus were Jim and Pattie Sumpter; Larry, Linda and Dorcas McConnell; Donnie and Glennie Helser; Betsy Dalton; Joe and Jane Sensibaugh; Glen and Bob Leake; Lamar Rogers; and Jay Clutter and his siblings.

101. On Detroit Street, our bus picked up Millicent and Nedra Horn; Mallory, Deanna and Billy Dederick; Dottie and Richard Campbell; and Max, Robert, Janet, and Nolan Huffer. In Lakeside Park, we picked up Dennis and Basil Blue; Ira Hyde and his brothers and sisters; Donnie and Geraldine Masterson; Sally and Bill Wyman; Merle and Jerry Harris; and Dane and Benny Joe Lane.

102. On Fox Farm Road, we picked up Bonnie, Norm, and Billy Grubbs; Doug Copeland, and Maynard and Orval Merica.

103. Some other boys who were my good friends in grade school were Tom Snell, Ira Hyde, Frank Tackett, Chane Funnell, John Kinch, and Larry Baker.

104. Other girls who were good friends in grade school were Sara Deafenbaugh, Nancy Lynn, Kathleen Fitzpatrick, Beverly Newby, Nancy Ingram, Connie Throckmorton, Patty Miller, Mallory Dederick, and Elaine Creakbaum.

105. Other great teachers in junior high school were Miss Voirol, Mrs. Spears, Miss Witham, and Miss Tuttle.

106. Other players on my freshman basketball team were Bruce Boley, Max Julian, Ward Kreigbaum, Les Konkle, and Larry Frauhiger.

107. Some of our other wonderful teachers in high school were Mary Reese, Delmer Bunnell, Lowell Knoop, Forrest Croop, David Middleton, Marie Love, Basil O'Reilly, and Giles Hoffer.

108. Some of our other great coaches were George Fisher, Bill Goshert, and Lew Goshert.

109. Other actors in *The Matchmaker* were Pauline Elliott and Sharron Duncan (who both played Dolly), Dave Delp, Bob Phillips, Bill Hoover, Don Pittenger, Steve Cartwright, Ward Kriegbaum, Alice Ann Manrow, Betsy Steele, Jerry Eaton, Sally Webb, Judy Hoffer, Katy Eggers, Lee Youse, Linda Croop, Sandi Adkinson, Ron Kay, Dallas Gusler, Richard Beers, Shawnee Ulery, Marita Shoemaker, Jean Westerman, and Lillian Bromberg. *The Matchmaker* later became the hit Broadway musical *Hello Dolly*.

110. Other teammates on my high school basketball team when I was a senior were Dick Lesh, Tom Knoop, Darrrell Phillips, Jack Cook, Paul Brown, and Jim McCleary.

111. Some other popular songs that we danced to at the sock hops were the "The Twist," "Queen of the Hop," "Kansas City," "Earth Angel," "Save the Last Dance for Me," "Oh Julie," "Great

Balls of Fire," "Lollipop," "Poor Little Fool," "Rock and Roll is Here to Stay," "Sweet Little Sixteen," "All Shook Up," "Love Me Tender," "Wake Up Little Susie," "Tutti Frutti," "Chantilly Lace," "Smoke Gets in Your Eyes," "You Send Me," "Sixteen Candles," "Twilight Time," and "It's Now or Never."

112. Some of my other classmates on the football team were Ward Kriegbaum, Bruce Boley, Larry Frauhiger, Tom Snell, Joe McKeigue, Les Konkle, Steve Cartwright, and Ted Dobbins.

113. Other guys who were good friends of mine in high school were Kevin Smyth, Bruce Boley, John Foresman, Larry Frauhiger, Ed Huffer, Bob Firestone, Steve Bochonok, Steve Cartwright, Monte Reece, Richard Beers, Steve Parsons, Denny Blue, Mike Munson, Randall Hopkins, and Jerry Eaton. Some girls who were good friends in high school were Pat Mulcahy, Kathy Fitzpatrick, Susie Lewis, Linda DePoy, Sandy Saemann, Lana Pinkerton, Marva McClure, Barb Hauth, Sally Webb, and Betsy Steele.

114. Mary Lee Willman, "Clark Gable & Others at Barbee," Accessed July 6, 2019, yesteryear.clunette.com.

115. Ibid.

116. Ibid.

Bibliography

Anglund, Joan W. *Childhood is a Time of Innocence*. New York, NY: Harcourt, 1964.

Atchison, Jack. *Simpler Times; Better Times: Growing Up in the 1940s and 1950s*. Atchison Publishing, 2012.

Barbee Hotel History (no author). Accessed July 6, 2019, barbeehotel.net.

Blake, Gary. *Does the Name Pavlov Ring a Bell?* New York, NY: Skyhorse Publishing, 2012.

Blazek, David. *Loose Parts*. Washington, DC: Washington Post Writers Group, (no date).

Borade, Gaynor. "Family Life in the 1950s: A Decade of Social and Economic Prosperity." Updated December 10, 2017, historyplex.com.

Bormet, Michelle J. *A History of the City of Warsaw, Indiana*. Kosciusko County Historical Society. Bourbon, IN: Harmony Visual Communications, 2001.

Burns, Adam. "Admiral." Accessed July 5, 2019, american-rails.com.

Child, Lydia Marie. "Over the River and Through the Wood," 1844.

City-Data Forum. "Growing up/Living in the Fifties." Accessed July 5, 2019, city-data.com.

Coplen, Dan. "A special kind of place: the Flag Pole custard stand was a Warsaw icon." Warsaw, IN: Kosciusko County Historical Society, 2006.

DePauw University yearbook. *The Mirage 1926*. Greencastle, IN: DePauw Junior Class, 1926.

Facebook public group. *Puns Galore*. Accessed 2018-19, m.facebook.com.

Facebook public group. *Punsters Anonymous*. Accessed 2018-19, m.facebook.com.

Facebook public group. *Punsters Asylum.* Accessed 2018-19, m.facebook.com.
Facebook public group. *The Merry Punsters.* Accessed 2019, m.facebook.com.
Facebook public group. *Unappreciated Puns.* Accessed 2018-19, m.facebook.com.
Facebook public group. *Unknown Punster.* Accessed 2018-19, m.facebook.com.
Hogan, Sally Coplen. *Kosciusko County Soap Box Derby.* Warsaw, IN: Kosciusko County Historical Society, 2014.
Indiana University yearbook. *The 1934 Arbutus.* Bloomington, IN: Undergraduates of Indiana University, 1934.
Johnson Smith and Company catalog. *Novelties.* Detroit, MI: 1950.
Kelly, Matthew. *The Biggest Lie in the History of Christianity.* North Palm Beach, FL: Blue Sparrow Books, 2018.
Livingston, A., May, B. and Foster, W. "I Tawt I Taw a Puddy Tat," 1950.
Klein, Fred. "Pennsylvania's Admiral, 1941-c1949." Modified in 2016, trainweb.org.
Major, Charles. *The Bears of Blue River.* New York, NY: Macmillan & Co., 1946.
McKay, Brett and Kate. "The Art of Manliness: Lessons in Manliness from Charles Atlas," Posted in 2011, artofmanliness.com.
Moger, Arthur. *The Complete Pun Book.* New York, NY: Ballantine Books, 1979.
Moger, Arthur. *The Best Book of Puns.* Secaucus, NJ: Citadel Press, 1988.
Raskin, Gene. "Those Were the Days," 1960.
Ringer, Robert. "The Age of Innocence." Posted November 26, 2015, robertringer.com.

Rowsome, Frank. *The Verse by the Side of the Road.* New York, NY: Plume, 1979.

Sand, Marguerite. "Inez Bolinger." Marjorie Priser. Posted in 1956, yesteryear.clunette.com.

Sand, Marguerite. "Local Father Is Wealthy Man." *Warsaw Times-Union.* Warsaw, IN: Reuben Williams & Sons, 1957.

Schmidt, H. and Jones, T. "Try to Remember,"1960.

Service, Robert. "The Shooting of Dan McGrew,"1907.

Snodgrass, Jerry. *Moments to Remember 1957: Teenage Life in the 1950s.* Denver, CO: Outskirts Press, Inc., 2008.

Symons, Mitchell. *That Book of Perfectly Useless Information.* New York, NY: HarperCollins, 2004.

Tennyson, Alfred Lord. "The Charge of the Light Brigade," 1854.

Van Osdol, Bill. *The Craig Boys: The Mystery of Gull Island.* Warsaw, IN: 1955.

Van Osdol, Marjorie L. Personal journal of Marjorie (Bolinger) Van Osdol, 1934-1963.

Van Osdol, Tom. *The Van Osdols Adventures: The Mystery of the Old Cellar.* Warsaw, IN: 1955.

Van Osdol, Tom. *The Craig Boys: The Mark on the Knife.* Warsaw, IN: 1955.

Warsaw High School yearbook. *Tiger.* Warsaw, IN: Reuben Williams & Sons, 1922.

Warsaw High School yearbook. *Tiger.* Warsaw, IN: Reuben Williams & Sons, 1931.

Whitman, Walt. *Leaves of Grass.* "There was a Child went Forth,"1855.

Wikipedia contributors. "Admiral Train." *Wikipedia, The Free Encyclopedia.* Accessed July 5, 2019, en.wikipedia.org.

Wikipedia contributors. "Bosco Chocolate Syrup."*Wikipedia, The Free Encyclopedia.* Accessed July 5, 2019, en.wikipedia.org.

Wikipedia contributors. "Captain Midnight." *Wikipedia, The Free Encyclopedia.* Accessed July 5, 2019, en.wikipedia.org.

Wikipedia contributors. "Charles Atlas." *Wikipedia, The Free Encyclopedia.* Accessed July 5, 2019, en.wikipedia.org.

Wikipedia contributors. "Necedah Shrine." *Wikipedia, The Free Encyclopedia.* Accessed July 5, 2019, en.wikipedia.org.

Willman, Mary Lee. "Clark Gable and others at Barbee." Accessed July 6, 2019, yesteryear.clunette.com.

William R. Van Osdol, MD

Postcard Reproductions

Barbee Hotel, Warsaw, Indiana
Bill Vukovich, race driver
Billy Sunday Tabernacle, Winona Lake, Indiana
Center Lake Beach and Park, Warsaw, Indiana
Center Lake Municipal Pavilion, Warsaw, Indiana
Center Street, Warsaw, Indiana
Chevrolet station wagon, 1959
Freezer Fresh ice cream truck
Little Pleasant Lake, Three Rivers, Michigan
McDonald Hospital, Warsaw, Indiana
Necedah, Wisconsin, Van Hoof farm
Pennsylvania Railroad Station, Warsaw, Indiana
Sacred Heart Catholic Church, Warsaw, Indiana
Union Station, Chicago, Illinois
University of Notre Dame Administration Building, Notre Dame, Indiana
University of Notre Dame Stadium, Notre Dame, Indiana
Wagon Wheel Playhouse, Warsaw, Indiana
Warsaw Armory, Warsaw, Indiana
Warsaw High School, Warsaw, Indiana
Warsaw Junior High School, Warsaw, Indiana
West Broad Street, Quakertown, Pennsylvania
Wildwood Resort, Bendon, Michigan, Sally Jo and Susan Jane
Wildwood Resort, Bendon, Michigan, Glen Eden cottage
Wisconsin Dells, Lone Rock, Lower Dells
Wisconsin Dells, Sugar Bowl, Lower Dells

A Time of Innocence

Made in the USA
Middletown, DE
01 October 2021

49071582R00209